CLITHEROE ABLAZE WITH GLORY

Clitheroe's Torchlight Processions

by

Sue Holden

Landy Publishing
1999

ISBN 1 872895 46 8

British Library in Cataloguing Publication Data.
A catalogue record of this book is available from the British Library.

Layout by Mike Clarke, 01254 395848

Printed by Nayler the Printer Ltd., Accrington, 01254 234247

Landy Publishing have also published:

Accrington Observed by Brian Brindle & Bob Dobson
Accrington's Changing Face by Frank Watson & Bob Dobson
An Accrington Mixture edited by Bob Dobson
Threads of Lancashire Life by Winnie Bridges
Lancashire, this, that an't'other by Doris Snape
Blackburn in Times Gone By by Jim Halsall
A Blackburn Miscellany edited by Bob Dobson
Blackburn's Shops at the Turn of the Century by Matthew Cole
Rishton Remembered by Kathleen Broderick
Lancashire Lingo Lines dialect poetry edited by Bob Dobson

A full list is available from:

Landy Publishing
'Acorns' 3 Staining Rise, Staining, Blackpool, FY3 0BU
Tel/Fax: 01253 895678

CONTENTS

FOREWORD

I was motivated to write this book by two things; the first was a wish to raise money for the Ainsworth Research Trust - a charitable trust set up by Cyril Ainsworth in 1997 which he hopes will encourage local people to write and publish historical material on the Ribble Valley area. The second was the realisation that a tradition which had been played out in Clitheroe with such style for over 100 years had never been documented other than in newspaper articles at the time.

My thanks go firstly to Cyril - his help at Clitheroe Library with various projects over the years has been invaluable and will go on benefitting the community for many years. His friendship and encouragement on a personal level are also of great importance to me.

Previous torchlight committees have worked incredibly hard to produce programmes of a very high standard - I am pleased to be able to reproduce extracts from them to a wider audience .

The Clitheroe Advertiser and Times over the years has reported in great detail the antics of the participants of the torchlight processions, and their reports have been of great assistance, both with the torchlight procession events and other local items included in the book.

Miss Sarah Ainsworth, Cyril's daughter very generously offered to provide financial backing in order that this book should be published. Her offer is greatly appreciated by the Ainsworth Research Trust, and by myself.

Lancashire Library's collection of photographs and programmes have been invaluable.

Thanks to the following people who loaned photographs: Messrs. John Wilmot, Keith Robinson, Roger Hargreaves, David Brooks, Tom Woods, Ronald Sellers, Philip Holgate, Mrs. Stella Wilson, Mrs. Belle Duckworth and Mrs. Chris Walmesley.

Thanks to fellow committee members of the Ainsworth Research Trust and the following individuals: Graham Claydon; the steward and members of Low Moor Club; Ribble Valley Borough Council for grant aid, and Roger Hirst.

Lastly, to my family who have been rather neglected whilst this book was being written.

Sue Holden
May 1999

INTRODUCTION

This year sees the 21st torchlight procession in the small Northern market town of Clitheroe. The tradition spans 112 years, and is Clitheroe's way of celebrating a major national event. Thus, occasions such as Coronations, Jubilees and Royal Weddings have all prompted the holding of a torchlight procession in the past. However, this is the first time one has been staged to herald the dawn of a new millenium. The torchlight processions have always attracted crowds of people from far and wide - Clitheroe is definitely on the tourist map and an event such as this is bound to attract many visitors to the town. It seems appropriate that a book explaining the history of the event should be published to coincide with this momentuous occasion.

An almost complete file of the official programmes is held at Clitheroe Library. They make fascinating and amusing reading, and many contemporary political and national events are alluded to by the use of poems and cartoons. The humour is almost always irreverent, and sometimes bawdy. The rhymes owe nothing to that great bard, William Shakespeare, but plenty to the wit of local people and I suspect to certain beverages which loosen the tongue and get the creative juices flowing! Clitheroe has apparently been known as a thirsty town since the 19th century, and it seems likely that it needed the lubrication in order to write the programmes for the torchlight processions. The butt of many of the jokes is government and its decisions, both local and national. Throughout are several recurring local traditions, well known to many 'Clitheronians', but maybe the background to some of these traditions is less well known even to local people. This book goes some way to explaining them so that today's children can learn about the traditions of their home town, and those people who read this who have no connections with Clitheroe can discover why the tradition has endured for so long. There can be few towns as small as Clitheroe that can boast of continuing such a tradition so often and so well.

These are the dates and reasons for the previous torchlight processions:

1887 Queen Victoria's Golden Jubilee

1893 Marriage of the Duke of York and Princess May of Teck.

1897 Queen Victoria's Diamond Jubilee.

1902 Coronation of Edward VII.

1911 Coronation of George V.

1923 Part of Castle War Memorial Fete.

1924 - do -

1935 Silver Jubilee of King George V and Queen Mary.

1937 Coronation of George VI.

1948 800th Anniversary of Borough of Clitheroe.

1951 Festival of Britain.

1953 Coronation of Queen Elizabeth II.

1960 No reason.

1965 Five years since last one.

1970 Five years since last one.

1973 Demise of Borough of Clitheroe.

1977 Queen Elizabeth II's Silver Jubilee.

1981 Marriage of Prince Charles to Lady Diana Spencer.

1986 800th Anniversary of the Castle.

1992 Queen Elizabeth II's 40 years on the throne.

BOROUGH OF CLITHEROE.

CELEBRATIONS of the SILVER JUBILEE of Their Majesties KING GEORGE V. and QUEEN MARY.

OFFICIAL PROGRAMME

(MORE OR LESS AUTHENTIC) OF THE

TORCHLIGHT PROCESSION

" Lux in tenebris "

SATURDAY EVENING, May 11th, 1935

CHIEF MARSHALS :

SIR H. RUSSELL HORNBY, BART.   W. HEATON, ESQ., J.P., M.H

COLONEL J. F. M. ROBINSON, M.C., T.D.   COUNCILLOR R. MANLEY.

Procession leaves Chatburn Road at 8-30 p.m.

ROUTE.

From Chatburn Road, via York Street, Market Place, Castle Street, Parson Lane, Bawdlands, Corporation Street, Eshton Terrace, Woone Lane, Primrose, Whalley Road, Moor Lane, Lowergate, Wilkin Street, Hayhurst Street, Shaw Bridge Street Duck Street, Waterloo Road, Well Terrace, to Waddington Road, and there disperse.

PRICE 2D.

Borough Printing Co., Ltd., York Street, Clitheroe.

GRAND FIREWORKS DISPLAY FROM THE CASTLE.

A gorgeous display of fire of every colour, procured at enormous expense and as the result of several personal visits to the Nether-Nether Land.

Opening—Signal Maroon, with Simultaneous Flight of Jubilee Rockets.
> Overheard : " Ooh, what a bang ! Bet that one cost 2d."

Ascent of Balloon, with Coloured Trailer.
> Seats now booking for the aerial flight to the " Suicide Hotel."

Snow-storm Streamers.
> Turn your collars up—summer is coming.

A Pyrotechnical Conglomeration.
> A polysyllabic " Big Noise."

Canopies of Jubilee Stars.
> Straight from Hollywood, not forgetting (h) Elstree.

Thunder and Lightning, preceding " Sky-Skrykers."
> We're letting off some of our pet demons.

Eruption of Cracker Mines.
> Every " cracker " contains a Jubilee souvenir.

Coloured Romans.
> Clitheroe's three L's. We know our Latin.

Peals of Thunder.
> The B.B.C. Forecast Department giving us a hand.

Stars—The Rivals of Venus.
> Shut yer eyes, Lizzie, I don't approve of these 'ere Nudists.

Shrapnel Barrage.
> You won't need tin helmets. It's one of " our's."

Dazzling Screen of Aerial Coruscations.
> Now's the time for a " daylight " snap.

Echoes of Lancashire Witches in the Emerald Castle.
> The Witches do pay us an occasional visit at the Castle.

Umbrellas of Fire.
> Look out for the rain of brimstone and treacle.

Asteroids, Chains, Tadpoles and Whistling Streamers.
> A fine collection of aerial freaks,
> Aerial wriggles and aerial streaks.

Thunderbolt Bombardment.
> From the Battle of " Waterloo."

A page from the programme for the 1935 Torchlight Procession which lists details of the firework display at the castle.

GETTING STARTED.

Once an event of sufficient importance is on the horizon, a torchlight procession is suggested to the Town Council. If the idea is accepted, a committee is formed of people who have been involved in the events over the years, and any other individual who it is felt could have a skill to offer or has expressed an interest in joining in. Fund raising is required in order to help with the cost of the programmes and advertising, also of course the all important torches and fireworks. An announcement is made through the local press of the date of the procession inviting entries, then some idea of the amount of support can be gained. This is the announcement made for the procession of 1902.

The programme is written by the committee once the entrants have submitted details of their float. Some things are regulars - the Low Moor Pig and the Bacon Eaters, the Carnival King and Queen with the Jester, and some local industries who appear every time. Floats are mainly on the backs of lorries begged and borrowed from different sources, and the construction of the tableaux is taken very seriously. Some are just humorous, others have a more serious message; but the main aim is to entertain the thousands of people who line the route of the procession. A lot of liquid refreshment is required and secreted in all sorts of unusual places, and by the end of the evening there could be some unplanned performances!

The torches are made of a huge hessian wick, dipped in non drip wax

and are made to burn for one and a half hours. In the very early days of the procession, they were made locally, but are currently being supplied from abroad. With the advent of motorised lorries with headlamps and electric street-lighting the need for torches diminished - in the early days 500 were given out and were still not sufficient; this year only 150 are being ordered. Official collectors are recruited to go around the route- in fancy dress - collecting donations from the crowd to offset the costs. Collection bags on long sticks were used to collect from the spectators in the upper windows of properties along the route, but this was abused by unauthorised collectors, so has had to be curtailed.

The route of the procession has had to be changed over the years to take into account the increased size of the lorries. The strarting point has varied - previously they have assembled in the George Street and Wilson Street area, with the numbers allotted to each lorry marked on the pavement - some of these still being visible. However as the lorries grew bigger they could not negotiate the narrow streets and tight bends so a change was made to assembling in Chatburn Road and this has continued. The torchlight procession committee meet with the police to discuss the safety of the route, and the best parking areas for visitors. Organisation of the event is carried out very conscientiously; the only thing that cannot be organised is the weather - lets hope that this year for this very special occasion the Gods are kind!

CORONATION FESTIVITIES.

It has been decided to have a Torchlight Procession on Saturday evening, the 28th June next. The Committee invite the assistance of the residents in the town and neighbourhood to make the Procession a success, not only by persons taking part in the Procession individually, but also by the organization of Mock Bands, Mock Corporations, and other Groups either on foot or on lurries.

The Committee will be glad to receive particulars as soon as possible of persons intending to join in the Procession either individually or in groups.

The Committee will provide Torches.

W. SELF WEEKS, Chairman.

C. HAMPSON. Hon. Sec.

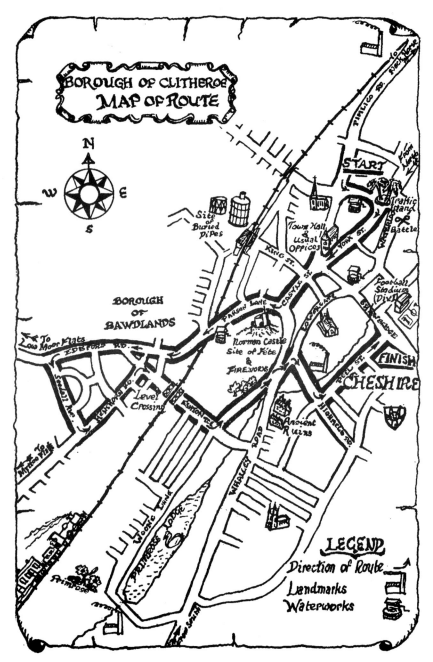

The route of the procession taken from the 1960 programme.

THE FIRST TORCHLIGHT PROCESSION

The occasion of Queen Victoria's Golden Jubilee in 1887 was considered a suitable occasion for Clitheroe to hold its first torchlight procession - after all this was the longest reign of any British queen, and the first national event worth celebrating in style for many years. Unfortunately no official programme exists for this event, and all attempts to track one down have failed. Luckily though, the *Clitheroe Times* of July 2nd 1897 reproduced the 1887 programme in full, so we are able to see a complete list of all the entrants. In addition, we have found a detailed newspaper account which appeared in the *Preston Guardian* of 1887, this being the newspaper which covered the Clitheroe area news at the time. Clitheroe's own newspaper came along the following year; in fact Clitheroe acquired not one but two weekly newspapers in 1888, the *Clitheroe Times* and the *Clitheroe Advertiser*. These two continued to be published weekly until 1920, when they were amalgamated to become - wait for it - *The Clitheroe Advertiser and Times and Low Moor, Chatburn and Ribblesdale Weekly Observer*. For obvious reasons this was later changed to the current title of *Clitheroe Advertiser and Times*.

The account in the *Preston Guardian* gives us a wonderfully detailed account of a whole weekend of celebrations commemorating the Golden Jubilee. The torchlight procession on the

---

TORCHLIGHT PROCESSION.

The arrangements for the torchlight procession on Saturday night were made by a special committee, with Councillor Garnett as chairman, and Mr. W. S. Weeks as secretary. The following programme was issued and carried out, with several additions :—

Four Horsemen.
The Members of the Clitheroe Bicycle Club.
Torchbearers on Foot.
The Band of the 2nd L.R.V
The Steam Fire Engine drawn by Four Horses and manned by the Fire Brigade exhibiting Fireworks and Coloured Fires.
Lurry with Firemen mounted on Piled Ladders Bearing Torches.
Torchbearers on Foot.
Horsemen two and two.
Torchbearers on Foot.
The Celebrated Prize Band of the Royal Black Match, as it appeared at Tel-el-Kebir.
Horsemen two and two.
Torchbearers on Foot.
Four Clowns on Horseback.
Torchbearers on Foot.
Jubilee Christy Minstrels on a Lurry, on their return from their Continental Tour, during which they appeared before several Crowned Heads.
Torchbearers on Foot.
Twelve Knights of the Cleaver Headed by their Chief.
Torchbearers on Foot.
A Lurry with Ethopians changing their Skins, under the influence of the Champion Soap.
Band of the Royal Cheshire Life Guards, under the Command of Colonel Blood, on his high mettled Steed.
Torchbearers on Foot.
Horsemen.
A Representative of John Bull and his Trades on a Lurry.
Daughters of Old England.
Torchbearers on Foot.
Horsemen.
Pluto, King of Hades, in his Chariot, drawn by his Horses of Darkness.
Arabs mounted on Jerusalem Ponies.
Torchbearers on Foot.

Saturday night was the climax of two days of celebrations, leaving Sunday free for religious observance of the event. A great deal of preparation had taken place, most of it by a group of officials of the town. Initially these were Mr. Tom Garnett, owner of Low Moor Mill and one of the town's biggest employers, Mr. William Self Weeks who was Town Clerk in later years, and Mr. Joseph Barrett who was the Borough Surveyor. Notices were posted around the town asking people who were interested in putting on a torchlight procession to a meeting at the Town Hall, at that time on the site now occupied by Clitheroe Library. We are told that there was a good response and many people joined together to make the event the success it was.

The Procession was held on 25th June and scheduled to begin at 10pm, but long before that the streets were thronged with people and almost impassable. Fancy dress was the order of the day, all of it made by the processionists themselves from whatever materials they could beg, borrow or acquire by other means! This of course would be the norm in 1887 - Marks and Spencers had not yet progressed as far as East Lancashire, and the drapers shops of the time would be places that few working class people could afford to buy from, unless for a special occasion. High fashion was restricted to the wives of the middle classes and the aristocracy. The processionists had of course to walk or ride on horseback to the assembly point, and it is reported that those taking part caused much amusement to the waiting crowds with their masks and costumes. The participants were to assemble in West's Yard, now the site occupied by D.J.P. Domestics and behind the then Brownlow Arms. This was the inn and coaching house kept by Billy West, later knocked down to make the entrance to King Lane wider, and on the site now occupied by the Yorkshire Bank. This was where all the travelling theatres, circuses and other amusements visiting the town used to be put. When they came to town the whole of Castle Street and Market Place used to be filled with stalls and amusements, and hundreds of people.

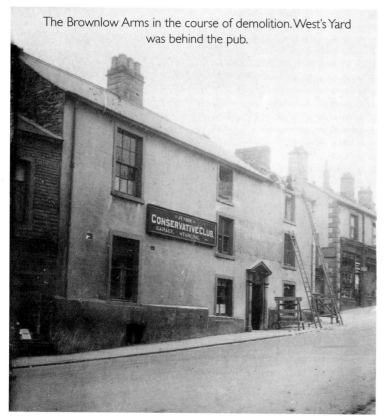

The Brownlow Arms in the course of demolition. West's Yard was behind the pub.

The First Procession Moves Off

As we can see from the programme, the procession was headed by four horsemen in grotesque costumes, followed by clowns with blackened faces bearing torches. Then came Lancashire Witches with broomsticks, an Australian rough rider and some Jubilee Christy Minstrels just back from a continental tour (although we are not told which continent!) Several bands feature in the procession, notably a band of Highland Pipers from Accrington, specially engaged for the occasion. At the time, Clitheroe had its own Volunteer Band, the prize winning Catholic Band, a Temperance Band, Primrose Band, and probably several more. Music making was one of the chief recreations, many instruments being handed down through families. Several local organisations would have their own band and all the churches would have music groups.

The Fire Brigade joined in with their steam fire engine acquired ten years previously. Prior to that they had to rely on the old manual engine which required twenty four men to operate the pumps, and carried a huge tank of water. This steam model was drawn by four horses and manned by the fire brigade letting off fireworks and showing coloured fire along the route. The horses must have had nerves of steel! The photograph opposite shows the Fire Brigade at a later procession proudly parading their steam engine.

The majority of the participants would be on foot, although a good number were on horseback. In fact the estimate in the newspaper account is that between 60 and 80 horsemen and around 400 persons took part. Imagine the scene in the streets of Clitheroe over 100 years ago - well before the introduction of electric street lighting of course. By 10pm all was in darkness. The procession made its way through the crowded streets, lit only by the flares and torches of the participants. It was reported that about 450 of these were handed out, many of them made at the local rope works of Mr. Henry Myers situated at Waterloo. The sound of the horses hooves rang on the cobbles, the odd spark flashing from them, all accompanied by the music of the assorted bands. The solid wheels of the lorries carrying the tableaux would be trundling along the uneven streets. The route which wound its way from Castle Street down Parson Lane, along Bawdlands to Eshton Terrace then round by Salford and Lowergate and back to Market Place via Waterloo and York Street, was lined with people several rows deep. The carnival atmosphere was punctuated by the sound of merriment and shouting as people recognised their friends and acquaintances through their masks and costumes. The newspaper reports that '*never in the memory of the oldest inhabitants has the ancient town of Clitheroe been so crowded as it was on this night*'. The parade ended about 11.30 pm, the participants exhausted but triumphant.

It is a credit to the town that a population of only 10,500 people as it was then could celebrate in such style, and amazing to think that such fun could be had with such limited resources as would be available then. The existence of a railway line connecting Clitheroe with towns such as Blackburn and Accrington and with many of the villages north of Clitheroe such as Chatburn, Gisburn and Hellifield meant that the crowds came from a wide area to witness the spectacle. and were able to join in the fun.

Clitheroe Fire Brigade outside the Fire Station then at the bottom of Moor Lane.

MOCK CORPORATIONS AND TORCHLIGHT PROCESSIONS

The living conditions of the 19th century provided an ideal background for the mock corporations which flourished in Northern England. They were particularly popular in areas which had a large proportion of underprivileged inhabitants and poor housing conditions, all of which applied to Clitheroe in the 19th century. For several years the tableaux of these mock corporations formed the bulk of the entries to the torchlight procession. The office of Mock Mayor and the election of officers to mock corporations was widespread, particularly in towns such as Clitheroe. Much pomp and circumstance was attached to the holding and electing of the bona fide Town Mayor, and a great deal of money spent on the feasts and regalia for the Mayor and members of the Corporation, whilst there were still many areas where people lived in substandard housing conditions. We know that the areas of Shawbridge, Bawdlands and Whalley Road, and the village of Low Moor had some of the poorest housing stock of the Borough.

Housing Conditions

This report from the Medical Officer of Clitheroe in 1890 details some of the surroundings: *'The older part of the town is indifferently built; many of the houses are low and have defective bedroom accommodation. In this class of property there are many back to back dwellings. In Clitheroe they amount to about 300, in Low Moor to 62. All houses so constructed are of necessity insanitary and ought to be promptly condemned by the local authority…I regret to say that in the Clitheroe portions of the urban sanitary district little has been done towards improving this class of property…'*. The contrast between the luxurious robes and regalia of the mayor, and the elaborate food consumed at its mayoral banquet, would be in stark contrast to the homespun clothing and monotonous diets of the residents of areas such as Bawdlands and Shawbridge, who understandably resented the trappings of the Mayor. So seriously was the idea of mock corporations taken that arches were constructed by the inhabitants to show when their territory was being entered. The arches constructed by some of the boroughs were splendid, particularly the Borough of Cheshire. Their arch was the turreted gateway of a castle upon which one could walk. This photograph shows the Shawbridge Arch constructed for the 1902 Procession. Don't forget that plywood and plastic had not yet been invented, so it must have weighed a ton!

These mock corporations often held their rowdy and disrespectful *'council elections'* around the time of the official mayor making ceremony, in an attempt to draw attention to the contrasts between the two events.

Cheshire Election

The *Clitheroe Advertiser* of 5th December 1890 gives a detailed account of such an election. It was the *'Ancient Borough of Cheshire'* (Shawbridge area) which was holding its mayoral election. No-one has yet come up with an explanation for the naming of Shawbridge as *'Cheshire'*. We are told that the election of the Lord Mayor the Rt. Hon. Col. Blood was followed by a banquet in his honour at the *'Town Hall'* and a *'Torchlight Procession'*. The Town Hall for the Borough of Cheshire was the Bridge Inn. Apparently a *'magnificent chain'* was presented to the Mayor and his corporation to be handed down to future generations. It would be interesting to find out what this consisted of - possibly scrap metal donated by a local blacksmith or a length of chicken wire. We are told of the procession following the election headed by the Band of

The Shawbridge Arch constructed for the 1902 procession.

bone of contention - the men who worked in the quarries were advised to bring home a few stones every night, the women to '*conserve their ashes and cockle and mussel shells and mixing these with a few clog irons and soles, distribute the mixture on the highway and bat it down with a fire shovel*'.

Lifeguards and a Lighthouse

The Royal Borough of Cheshire was the most active and the largest of the Mock Corporations; it mimicked almost all of the towns facilities and added a few of its own. It had a borough barber, blacksmith, life guards, baker, hospital, and police force to name but a few, all of whom turned out for the torchlight processions. By 1897 it had awarded itself a Town Clerk and a mounted police force. It even had its own mounted cavalry, although they were reported to be '*generally on foot and sometimes on the feet of other people…and several of the army have grown corns on their toes*'. The Band of the Royal Cheshire Life Guards played the carol of Cheshire:

the Royal Cheshire Life Guards in full regalia. Also featured were '*replicas of the amenities*' provided by the Corporation in the form of a tin bath, foot square playgrounds etc. The tin bath was a dig at the council who were refusing to provide public baths for the town. The condition of the streets in the area was obviously a

With hen farms and chickens and thousands of eggs
And looms full of beams and whisky in kegs,
A brewery to brew us good ale without measure
There's naught in the world to compare with old Cheshire.

There was of course a brewery next to the Bridge Inn at this time. Colonel Blood has awarded himself the K.G.B., showing a bit of one upmanship; the Mayor of Clitheroe at the time was plain old Alderman Garnett! Due to the existence of Brewery Mill lodge in 'Cheshire' (near the houses on the new Highmoor Park Estate but now drained and grassed over) the Borough had found it necessary to erect a lighthouse and have a lifeboat, in case anyone got into difficulties. There were a few teething problems however as the bright light was disturbing the neighbouring hen farms so the plan was to move it to nearby Peel Park. Finally Cheshire paraded its own Cottage Hospital, farmyard, butcher, baker, school and executioner! Each one of these had a tableaux on the back of a lorry; the one representing Read and Embleys shoeing forge actually had a working forge with shoeing taking place as it moved! I wonder what the European regulations responsible for ruining our Christmas lights would have made of that one!

Clitheroe's Water Supply

Another source of discontent at the time is parodied in the newspaper account concerning the Cheshire election. It is reported that samples of the water from the brook bordering the territory were taken by the Mayor. This was Mearley Brook, said to divide the Borough of Cheshire from the Borough of Waterloo (now the area of Tesco and the inner bypass). Analysis was reputed to show that the water contained 14% of refuse and 21% of animal fat. No surprise, since the areas north of the town such as Worston all used Mearley Brook as a drain for their sewage. Reference is then made to the Corporation being short of somewhere to put their refuse now the brook was not to be used, so they were informed of the bottomless pit which had been excavated about 3 years before in the search for water (actually a new reservoir) The background to these allegations refers to the stormy path travelled in obtaining a clean water supply for Clitheroe - fierce arguments continued for several years in the 1850s with local men of influence having opposing views. Those in favour wanted to start a private company to provide the supply, those against felt that the supply should belong to the Corporation, and not to private individuals. At the time water was supplied

by the three wells in the town, with some houses having their own private pump, and an odd well in other properties. A hawker used to go around with a donkey and cart selling water at two cans for a penny. Many people felt that the Corporation were negligent in their maintenance of the Town's Well so a sample was analysed professionally and found to be of inferior quality and it became obvious that a fresh supply was needed. Added to this was a government report on the sewerage and drainage of the town which found Clitheroe 'seriously wanting on all counts'. It found that 'the present drainage was utterly inefficient and the water supply quite inadequate'. So eventually the Clitheroe Waterworks Act of 1854 was passed and construction of a new reservoir up on West Bradford Fell was begun. Ownership of the Waterworks passed to the Corporation in 1877 from the private company who instigated it, and Clitheroe was supplied with a reliable supply of clean water at last.

OTHER BOROUGHS

Whalley Road

Whilst the Borough of Cheshire was the largest and most vocal of the Mock Corporations, the Whalley Road area also had its own borough and officers as can be seen from entries in the processions over the years. In 1897 the Borough of Salford, Russell St and Woone Lane had Robert Bowker as its Mayor, and they could boast a water bailiff and a vaccination officer! This last was a reference to the vaccination campaign running at the time to try to combat the various epidemics which were due largely to overcrowding and poor sanitation; people were actually brought before a court for not having their children vaccinated.

In the *Clitheroe Advertiser* of 3rd November 1950 there is a report of the 90th birthday of Dr. J. Cowperthwaite a former 'Mayor' of Whalley Road. He claims to have been the only 'Mayor' to have been taken round the town on a wagon drawn by six horses. Opposite is a photograph of the Russell Street arch built for the 1902 Procession. Russell Street was part of what is now named Whalley Road. In 1923 the

Russell Street's Arch in 1902. Russell Street later became part of Whalley Road.

Waterloo's Arch in 1902.

Borough of Whalley Road was still in evidence, boasting of its 'hen pens' reference to a lot of allotments behind the houses where many people kept hens to supplement their diet and their incomes.

Waterloo

The Borough of Waterloo was the neighbouring borough to Cheshire, divided from it by a '*river*' better known as Mearley Brook. Although not much is known about its '*officers*' this verse in the 1897 programme proclaimed its qualities:

We've plenty of lime and we've plenty of mills
And we know where there's green peas and duck!
We never seek physic and we never want pills
While we've got both a brewery and brook.

The Borough of Waterloo's chariot in 1897 was occupied by Squire Birch as its Mayor, and it also had its own band, police force, butcher, baker, blackguard (unnamed) followed by an assortment of devils of different colours! By 1923 the Boroughs of Waterloo and York Street had amalgamated and re-enacted the Battle of Waterloo around the '*big lamp*' - this referred to the gas street lamp positioned as it was then in the middle of the road at Waterloo. Recently there was a bid to return the '*big lamp*' as it was always known locally, to its original site, as the top of the original lamp had been recovered from the tip. It is now back in Waterloo at the side of the road just before the 'Royal Oak' pub.

Bawdlands

Bawdlands was elevated to the status of a County Borough for the purposes of the torchlight procession. Their Mayor was Sir Mark Wildman who seemed to need to conceal his identity by using a pseudonym. He did however allow the sewage farm to provide '*tastefully arranged samples...green side up*'. By 1897 the sewage farm had been in existence for two years and a sideline from the sewage works was the sale of various grades of corn grown on the site as we can see from this advert from the ***Clitheroe Advertiser***. In 1902 Bawdlands had its own entry, and its heartfelt lament featured in the programme is as follows:

Stinkle, stinkle little sewer
You are anything but pure.
It matters not where e'er you are,
You can smell it near or far.

The sewering of Clitheroe was obviously not being completed to everyone's satisfaction! Overleaf is the lavish arch constructed by Bawdlands for the 1902 procession.

Sale by Auction

CLITHEROE SEWAGE FARM

TO BE SOLD by Auction, by Mr. Amos Duerden, at the Cattle Market, Clitheroe, on Monday, the 19th day of August, 1895, at 11-0 o'clock in the forenoon, in the following or such other lots as may be determined at the time of sale, and subject to conditions of sale to be then produced, and which may be inspected at the Town Clerk's Office three days before the sale.

Lots 1, 2, and 3—The CORN growing on the Corporation Sewage Farm, at Henthorn near Clitheroe. The Corn field covers an area of about five acres and the corn will be offered in three nearly equal lots, as marked out by pegs.

Lot 4—The FOG and WINTER EATAGE from the 1st September to the 25th March next, of the Meadows at the said Sewage Farm.

Lot 5—The WINTER EATAGE from the 1st September to the 25th March next, of the Pastures at the said Sewage Farm.

Mr. Robert Carter, farm bailiff, Henthorn, will show the various lots, and for further particulars apply to the Auctioneer, or to
 JOHN EASTHAM, Town Clerk
Clitheroe, 6th August, 1895.

Parson Lane

As part of the Royal Borough of Parson Lane's entry in 1911, Staggerum's menagerie were exhibiting a '*fine bred Lion*' - Castle King (*if he was much finer you would not be able to see him*). '*The Cracker*' was a Bengal Tiger captured at the top of Rock Street, '*Shiveram*' was a famous spotted leopard, spotted in the Cattle Market and to complete the Menagerie was '*Huggeram*' captured at the top of the Castle Pole. These wild animals, under the control of that daring famous trapper Paul Karagouzel, gave a display of their fearsome antics which, by all accounts, was side splitting. In 1923 Parson

Bawdlands Arch in 1902

Lane had its borough representatives - headed by Tarzan - as you will see from the photograph overleaf taken outside the Railway View Inn. Tarzan was regularly refreshed by glasses of beer through the hole in his chest.

Wilkin

The Borough of Wilkin now better known as the Highfield Road area and an area of very poor housing assembled five lorries for the 1911 procession. It boasted the presence of Adam and Eve in Wilkin Gardens; these gardens were celebrated, according to the programme, for the production of the tobacco from which are made the *'Adam & Eve'* brand of cigars - *'once you've had 'em, you heave!'* Also on a biblical theme Cain and Abel are in their shaving and haircutting saloon - no advance in their prices but the treatment is as *'barbarous'* as ever. Their comb was a garden rake and the scissors a pair of shears! These tableaux in addition to the *'Black Dyke Band'* of 36 performers and a lifeboat, was a considerable showing from an area where poverty and sub-standard housing was the norm.

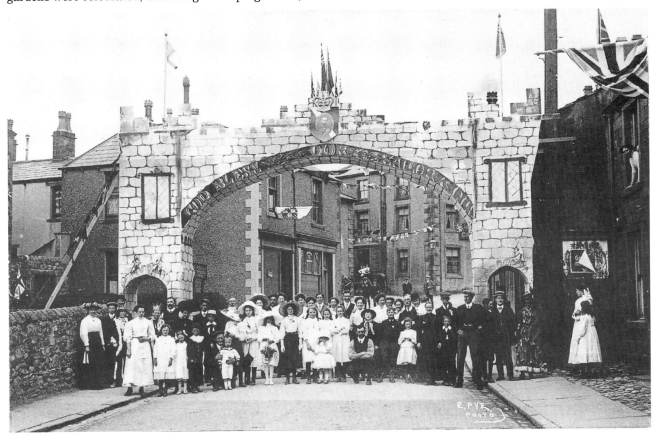

The Parson Lane Arch in 1902 with some of the residents of the area.

'Tarzan' outside the Railway View Inn in 1923. Note the bottle being aimed at the hole behind which is the mouth of the wearer of the costume!

Worston Corporation

In contrast to the reasons for the existence of the 'Boroughs' in Clitheroe, the formation of a 'Corporation' in Worston is a little less obvious. Worston had less than 100 inhabitants, yet its tradition of Mock Mayor was continued until the 1990s. Reports in the newspaper of 1894 identify the Calf's Head as being the Mayor's Parlour. Election promises were creative to say the least. The newly installed

Mayor of 1894, 'Alderman' John Barnes promised to sewer the Borough by boring a tunnel through Crow Hill. He also contemplated laying an electric tramway to Whalley and lighting Worston by electricity. His piece de resistance was to suggest that the brook through Worston might be made navigable from Preston, and if this could be achieved 'the farmers could swim their pigs right into the Borough from

Carlisle, thus saving the expense of railway carriage'. It would appear that some of these promises owed their origins to the copious amounts of ale being consumed in the '*Mayor's Parlour*'! The *Clitheroe Advertiser* of 24th September 1965 included a photograph of the Corporation of Worston complete with Mayoral Party on a carriage outside Middlewood, the home of Mr. and Mrs. W. King Wilkinson. The photograph is understood to have been taken in 1897 on the occasion of Queen Victoria's Diamond Jubilee. They had the honour of leading the procession in 1897.

What seems incredible about all this, is not that these Boroughs existed - indeed, there seems ample justification for a little light relief in the shape of poking fun at the Corporation and its officers; but that the local newspaper devoted such a lot of space to '*reporting*' the spoof goings-on. They explain in the obituary of George Speight in 1919, the importance of a man known as '*Col. Blood*' or '*Mayor of Cheshire*', and how Cheshire always led the way in the torchlight procession. '*Col. Bloods*' arrival back from London by rail was reported to have been '*met by a donkey cart and a crowd of several thousand cheering him - though at the same time laughing at the incongruity of it all!*' This probably sums up the whole tradition - although it was played along with and even encouraged - all along the participants knew that it wasn't for real.

The photograph of the Worston Corporation of 1897 published in the *Clitheroe Advertiser*. Unfortunately, it is of very poor quality.

TORCHLIGHT TRADITIONS

Low Moor and its Bacon Eaters

This procession sees the first appearance of the banner made for Low Moor and its Ancient Order of Bacon eaters, with their motto : 'We love bacon'. The Low Moor contingent was so called as it was said that everyone along St. Paul's Street kept a pig in a sty at the bottom of the garden, and the inhabitants lived on the bacon that resulted from the killing of the animals. The banner pictured opposite was made by Tom Robinson of Low Moor, and painted at a later date by Elijah Bolton. Elijah was an expert photographer who took to painting his subjects during the winter months when the weather stopped his photography work. He was born in Sabden, but worked at Low Moor Mill as a half timer and was paid two shillings and sixpence a week, or twelve and a half pence in decimal currency. As you can see, the banner is superbly painted with pictures of pigs, a different picture appearing on each side. It has appeared in every procession since 1902.

Pig's Progress

1911 sees the first appearance of the now famous, 'Low Moor Pig'. The theme of Low Moor being 'We love bacon' it seems fitting that they should parade a pig, the subject of their affections. This pig has appeared in every Low Moor entry of the torchlight procession ever since.

Percy, the Low Moor Pig.

Christened 'Percy' he was originally a whole stuffed boar, provided I am told by Bud Howard the Low Moor butcher. The boars head was mounted on a wooden body with wheels by Mr. Tom Jackson a master carpenter whose premises were on King Street on the site of the Apricot Meringue and Orchid Bridal Designs. This hollow body has the added advantage of being able to store supplies of liquid refreshment to sustain the Bacon Eaters! In 1923 The Urban District Council of Low Moor is still much in evidence, proudly parading Percy and their beautiful banner. The programme for this year gives the pig's age as 2000 years - I've seen this pig at very close quarters, and it could well be true!

1935 is the first year that all the mock corporations disappear, although Low Moor is still represented by the pig and the banner, in fact this year the pig is 2012 years old! Surprisingly, no reference is made to the sale of Low Moor Mill and the associated houses which took place in 1930, although its effects would surely still be being felt. Not only had their biggest employer gone, but their houses were sold off to different landlords. In 1937 the Low Moor Urban District Council still appears as a separate entity, referring to its banner as having been painted by 'Elijah of old', as described earlier.

The pigs age is in reverse; last time it was 2012 this year only 1002, and dated by her snout (hopefully not by the number of rings through it!) It has been the recipient of *'intensive monkey gland treatment'* and by the next procession will be a suckling pig! In 1951 *'His Porkship'* makes his appearance with the bacon eaters, back to eating their fill of bacon after the period of rationing after the war is finally ended. Such is their devotion to their mascot that they didn't even consider eating him to satisfy their cravings - I wonder why! He has continued to be the subject of many a rhyme ever since.

Waterworks Inspection

The annual Waterworks Inspection was a very serious affair carried out by member of the Corporation and the Waterworks Committee. The custom was begun when the Town took over the responsibility for the Waterworks, and it was deemed necessary that members of the council should inspect the workings annually. It is difficult to imagine that the occasion really required all these dignitaries, much less the lavish hospitality which followed, although it did provide good fodder for the programmes! In the report of the 1926 inspection, a total of 27 local dignitaries made the trip up to

The two sides of the Low Moor banner, beautifully painted by Elijah Bolton.

the reservoirs on Grindleton and West Bradford Fells ferried in a convoy of motor cars. The photograph shows the party outside the bungalow; an official photograph being taken at each trip, paid for of course from the public purse! Twenty three springs were yielding 800,000 gallons per day, and it was claimed that Clitheroe probably had the best supply of water in the country. After the inspection, lunch provided by the Swan and Royal Hotel was taken at the bungalow erected for the Waterworks. Many toasts were proposed and I bet they weren't water! The Waterworks Inspection comes in for more criticism in 1935; it was particularly resented at this time as the Means Test was introduced in 1932 and many people locally were finding their unemployment benefit cut so that they could barely feed their families, yet here was a bunch of local businessmen going on a jamboree funded by the ratepayers, just to look at the water supply. Why could they not just turn a tap on and pass a cup round? Surely the taste of the water, and its prescence when the taps were turned, was proof enough that the works were

functioning correctly. In 1960 Clitheroe Waterworks was the subject of one of the floats, motto *'nil amalgamatum'* referring to moves afoot to amalgamate them with the Fylde Water Board. The tradition of the *'Waterworks Picnic'* or more politely *'Annual Waterworks Inspection'* was wearing very thin by now, and the extract from the following poem from the 1960 programme says it all:

OUR MAGNIFICENT WATERWORKS
No wonder that our council kind
A need to celebrate did find,
And then a thought came to their aid-
If annual inspection must be made,
Why not combine this routine matter
With pints of ale and a well filled platter;
And on their pilgrimage did take
A picnic hamper in the brake
Long years have passed and times have changed,
But still this picnic is arranged,

The official party at the waterworks inspection of 1926. This event was also commonly known as the Waterworks Picnic.

But then they've more to celebrate
(Two boreholes pump at a steady rate),
And they can toast in old and mild
An Undertaking unde-Fylde.

The tradition was maintained until 1962, when Clitheroe lost control of its own water supply to the Fylde Water Board. The final Waterworks Inspection was carried out on March 27th 1963 amidst even more pomp and ceremony than usual. At a meeting of the council prior to this a Councillor had called it '*a jaunt*' much to the annoyance of the Waterworks Committee. He claimed that of the people attending the Inspection only 50% ever attempted to inspect the workings, the rest going straight to Pinewood, the bungalow erected at the site where the refreshments were served. He seems to have voiced a lot of other people's opinions.

Clitheroe Gas Works Creations

1951 sees the first appearance of the legendary Gas Works Dragon - a monster so startling that many people still remember it. As the photograph shows it was a fearsome looking monster, made at Clitheroe Gas Works by some of the men employed there, one of whom was Mr. Ronald Sellers who can remember the engine which powered it breaking down as they set off, so leaving them no alternative but to pump the petrol through by hand to keep it going! This bright green dragon paraded in the procession breathing out flames from its jaws and

must have been a sight to behold. Apparently it was so tall that on its way round someone had to lift the bunting threaded across the streets out of its way!

In 1957 the Gas Works Dragon was having a well earned rest, but was replaced by the '*Gas Works Giant*'. As you can see from the photograph this creation was on the scale of the dragon, and had someone in the head watching out for obstacles. A new invention in 1960 was the Gas Works Dalek, pictured here. Inspired by the new children's T.V. programme '*Doctor Who*' the dalek was the creation of the B.B.C., imitated by Clitheroe Gas Works. Its predecessor, the Gas Works Dragon was '*slain*' in 1962, sadly for such a splendid creation it had finally to be dismantled and scrapped. The Dalek was a smaller affair, and very topical, though not built in Clitheroe. It was propelled by a small mechanical shovel part, and moved along with flashing lights through the procession. Its driver was Mr. Ronald Sellers, manager of the Gas Works at the time, and '*Dr. Who*' in the form of Mr. Harold Hammond of the Gas Works accompanied it with Mr. Alan Grainger acting as '*pilot*'.

The famous 'Gas Works Dragon', built for the 1951 Torchlight Procession.

The Gas Works 'Dalek'.

The Gas Works Giant and some of the workers who helped to build it.

OVER THE YEARS

1893 was the year of the marriage of the Duke of York and Princess May of Teck and as the procession for the Golden Jubilee of Queen Victoria was such a success it was decided to repeat it. This year we have a copy of the original programme in addition to the newspaper report.

In 1893 the local newspaper was a fairly restrained affair - the report was of a '*Monstre torch-light procession*'. The organisation of this was attributed to Mr. W. Self Weeks, who was Town Clerk from 1909 to 1934 and a local solicitor. His contribution to the history of Clitheroe is legendary - he wrote *Clitheroe in the 17th century* published in 1905. Stephen Clarke wrote *Clitheroe in its Coaching Days* in 1897 and *Clitheroe in its Railway Days* in 1900, but neither of these works, although fascinating, covers the early development of Clitheroe in as much detail. Weeks has based much of his writing on the Court Rolls and other Borough Records of the Honor of Clitheroe. Arthur Langshaw has since added to our knowledge of Clitheroe's past in detail, but Weeks is credited with the first published insight into Clitheroe's early history.

An interesting fact reported about Clitheroe is that there were two cycling clubs in the town in 1893 not only was there a Clitheroe Cycling Club whose members in the procession numbered about 30 or 40, but there was also a Clitheroe Temperance Cycling Club, with a similar number of members riding. I wonder if the members of the former club were wobbling a little at the end of the evening! Clitheroe was always known as a thirsty town, on account of its having a large number of pubs in relation to the number of inhabitants. As an antidote to this, the Temperance Movement was well supported in Clitheroe in the 19th century with many people signing the pledge. In fact, in 1864 the Temperance movement was responsible for erecting the water fountain which stood in the Market Place, pictured here where the library now stands. Worston's Mock Corporation was appearing in 1893, as were the

The drinking fountain in the Market Place erected by the Temperance Movement in 1864. This photo was taken before the building of the Library in 1905.

'*Waddington Snowdrop Minstrels*'. We even had a lifeboat all the way from Upbrooks - which maybe tells us something about the drains (or lack of them!) Bawdlands problems with sewers seems to have begun too - they already had a '*Bawdlands Main Sewer Prize Band*' whose new tune was '*The Ground is sinking still*'. In the February of 1893 there was a government enquiry into the proposal by the Borough to purchase land for a sewage farm at Henthorn and to borrow the sum of £20,450 to carry out the works. A lot of detailed discussion took place about the relative merits of the types of pipe and treatment of the effluent, all faithfully reported by the newspaper. Much of the pipework ran through Bawdlands and caused severe disruption to the inhabitants.

This procession was reported to have been almost a mile in length and lit up from end to end by hundreds of flaming torches - it must have been quite a sight!

Queen Victoria's Diamond Jubilee

1897 saw the Diamond Jubilee of our longest serving Queen to date - Queen Victoria. The success of the processions in 1887 and 1893 had whetted the townsfolks appetite for torchlit celebrations and another one was staged. Each programme seemed to get bigger and better than the last and each procession bigger than its predecessor as people entered into the spirit of the occasion. This period of time seems to have been the hey-day of the Mock Corporation, and pride of place this year was given to Worston with its '*Mayor*' Alderman Sir John Finch, who according to the 1891 census lived in a cottage next to the Calfs Head with his wife, and was a platelayer on the railway.

Low Moor was an Urban District in 1897, so had no Mayor, just a Colonel Mass, O.B.E., mounted on his '*celebrated Jerusalem Pony*'. The Low Moor lilt was:

We have a model village, and we are a model crew,
We have no licence - off or on - but this is what we do;
Whenever we feel thirsty, and wish a drink to try
We just step o'er our boundary and find two pubs close by.

Low Moor is still without its own pub although the Club now has a licence.

The back page of the programme tells us that trains leave at 11.14 pm for Hellifield and intermediate stations, and for Blackburn and places en route at 11.30 pm. Obviously people travelled from far and wide even then to witness the torchlight procession - these trains seem to have been specially laid on for the occasion.

Ox Roast

Whilst not strictly speaking a feature of the torchlight procession, two tickets for an ox roast have survived, which was a part of any major celebrations in Clitheroe. The ticket reproduced here is numbered 1231, although we do not know how many were sold. A ballot for the ox took place the day before the roast, entitling the holder to have the head cured and mounted, on the understanding that the body of the ox would be presented to the members of the ox roast committee for general distribution. The holder of the winning ticket was Miss Amy Halliwell - I wonder if the head has survived and is decorating the wall of a house in Clitheroe? It is reported that from 3 am on the Saturday the ox had been '*amusing itself being roasted in the cattle market*', and that a great many people came and helped to baste it. Presumably vegetarians were unheard of at this time in Clitheroe, the newspapers turn of phrase being a little indelicate here! The Mayoress, Mrs. Garnett had the honour of cutting the first slice at 3.30pm on the Saturday after the ox had been presented to the ox roast committee by Miss Halliwell. She used a pair of Diamond Jubilee

1231 QUEEN   **DIAMOND**

VICTORIA'S   **JUBILEE 1897.**

Ox-Roasting Celebration at Clitheroe,

JUNE 25th and 26th, 1897.   **6d.**

A Draw will take place in connection with this Celebration, and the holder of the Ticket which bears the winning number, will be presented with the Head and Horns of the Ox (mounted,) and be regarded as the donor of the feast. Time and place of the Draw and winning number will be duly announced in the Clitheroe Advertiser and Clitheroe Times.

This Ticket admits the holder to witness the roasting, and in the distribution of the Ox, preference will be given to Ticket Holders.   [Whewell, Printer.

Members of the Ox Roast Committee of 1887. They were, from the left rear: J. Bibby (Landlord of the New Inn), G. Walmesley (Shoemaker), J. Cowman (Butcher), J. Bleazard (Contractor), S. Speak (of Salthill Road), Young Lofthouse (Master of the Workhouse), J. Harrison (Sadler), J. Crabtree, Edmund ?. Seated: Fred Brown (Tailor), G. Whewell (Printer), J. Norcross.

carvers, while the Mayor cut the second slice with the carvers used at the Coronation of Queen Victoria in 1838. All this was watched by huge crowds of people, who all received a slice of meat afterwards. The photograph is of the ox-roast committee of 1887.

The 1897 celebrations also saw the presentation to the town of a magnificent gold Mayoral Chain, presented by Ald. Thomas Garnett. He was anxious that the chain should always be used for the purpose it was intended rather than meet the fate of regalia in other towns and be sold off, so he presented it to be held in trust for the Corporation. The chain is still used by the Mayor of Clitheroe.

Queen Victoria reigned for a further four years after the procession celebrating her Diamond Jubilee. Her death in 1901 saw the end of the Victorian era - the longest reign of any British queen. The Victorian era in Clitheroe saw the rapid expansion of the town - the arrival of the railway in 1850 improved communications with other nearby towns. The mills in the area grew and prospered, some falling by the wayside, but other industries springing up to replace them. Over the Victorian era the population of the town rose from 6,000 to 11,500 according to the census figures - that's almost doubling itself in the space of 60 years. Ninety years later at the 1991 census it was still only just over 13,000.

What must it have felt like to live in a time of such rapid growth and development?

Edwardian Processions

The Coronation of King Edward V11 in June 1902 gave Clitheroe another chance to hold a weekend of celebrations, crowned by a *'Monstre Torchlight Procession'*. This took place on August 9th 1902, celebrations for the Coronation having been delayed due to the imminent ending of the Boer War, also in June. Clitheroe had sent 140 men to the Boer War (according to the newspaper this was the highest percentage of any Lancashire town) and had incurred several casualties, so the preceding few years would have been overshadowed by worry for many local families.

The Borough of Cheshire takes its usual prominent position in the torchlight procession; there is now a new Mayor Sir John Speedy, who has joined forces with the Mayor of Wilkin. Wilkin is the area of town next to Shawbridge, or *'Cheshire'*. These areas consisted of many small back to back houses lived in by poor families many of them working at the mills. The lives of the people living here would be temporarily enlivened by the events of the Coronation and the local festivities. We have to remember that their day would begin very early with lighting of fires and drawing water, then off to work for the most part in the mills. A working day would be very long, hard, noisy and probably dirty. Food would be adequate but diets would be monotonous and based largely on vegetables, eggs if they had land available for chickens, but with only occasional meat. Lighting in the houses would be by gas lamps, and that only in the main rooms; candles would still be extensively used. Spare time would be limited, but any excuse for fun in a community living in such close proximity to each other would be eagerly grasped.

According to the procession programme the Borough of Cheshire had *'Boers and Britains fraternising'*. The cottage hospital which appeared in the procession was being offered to the Corporation of Clitheroe for use as a smallpox hospital. Smallpox was on the increase again, and the Borough of Clitheroe was looking for a site upon which to build an isolation hospital. However they must have turned down the Cheshire

offer as the *Clitheroe Advertiser* in January 1903 reports that a site was allocated at Salthill for an isolation hospital and building was completed at a cost of £300, plus the cost of the ambulance cart of £100. The hospital was built on land tenanted by a farmer upon whom considerable pressure was brought to bear before he could be persuaded to give up his land, although he was recompensed by the sum of £20! The hospital appears on the 1912 Ordnance Survey map to the rear of the Workhouse and between the quarries of Salthill and Bellman - suitably isolated from other dwellings.

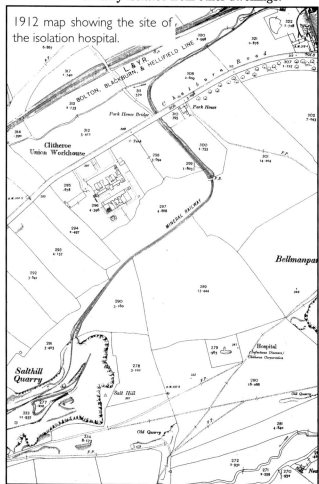

1912 map showing the site of the isolation hospital.

Education

The Cheshire area mentions its school in the 1902 programme, which is to be *'established to take advantage of the proposed new Education Act'*. This brief mention refers to the 1902 Education Act, at the time the most important change to education locally. Over the year there had been a lot of heated debate reported in the paper, and a lot of opposition from church officials. The Act sought to establish a non-denominational system of secondary education over the country. Currently the churches had control over most of the schools, thus were able to use the schools to promote their religious ideals. They saw the proposed *'board schools'* as requiring them to pay rates and taxes to fund schools whose ideals they did not necessarily agree with. There were many arguments nationally over this issue before the Balfour Act as it was known became law. Attendance at secondary school would become more widespread and mandatory; the programme points out that boys will now be required to attend school on Wednesday afternoons instead of caddying at the Golf Links! The Golf Club established in 1891 was obviously providing useful extra pocket money for teenage boys who saw no competition between the school room and caddying! The money was probably a valuable addition to the household finances; the Workhouse or *'Coplow'* as it was

Market Place Arch, 1902.

Chatburn Road Arch, 1902. These triumphal arches were all over the town. The houses on the right would have been very recently built in 1902.

known was a real threat for many working class families.

The torchlight procession had a lucrative spin-off for one local business at least. It was reported at the meeting of the torchlight committee on April 28th that an order for two hundred torches should be placed with Mr Theo Wilson an ironmonger and tin plate worker of York Street, whose tender was the lowest. There was also the offer of a loan of torches by Clitheroe and Whalley cricket clubs. Firework manufacturers were also being sought this year for the first time and Mr. M. Duckett was charged with the job of finding out who could offer the most suitable rockets at the best price. The castle was to be used for '*fusing*' coloured fire and Dr. A. Musson was given the job of trying to get a searchlight to illuminate the keep. The fireworks display was to be on the Thursday night, the night of the Coronation. Local opinion was that although the 1902 procession was not the biggest, it was the best equipped and managed of any so far. This was the year that the triumphal arches erected for the boroughs seem to have proliferated as illustrated previously. Even Market Place, not a heavily populated area, had an arch.

The reign of Edward VII was very short in comparison to that of his mother, Queen Victoria. He died of pneumonia on May 6th 1910, only 9 years after being crowned, and on May 7th, his brother George V took his oath as king, being crowned on June 22nd.

1911

From the report in the *Clitheroe Advertiser* of the 1911 procession it would seem that the summer of 1911 was similar to that of 1998 - wet! Only *'strong optimism and the knowledge that their plight could not be worse kept the processionists going'*.

The amount of effort put into the tableaux seems immense, considering how hard daily life was. This photograph shows the arch constructed by Bawdlands for this years festivities; a completely different one from the 1902 construction.

The *Clitheroe Times* reports on the splendid efforts made by the town to decorate their surroundings.

> The main thoroughfares in the town are gay with a profusion of flags and bunting. while many shopkeepers have taken considerable trouble and expense in the decoration of their premises. But the adornment of the streets is not confined to any one quarter of the town. Everywhere is to be seen the Union Jack, pictures of the King and Queen, and paper festoons add colour and effect to the whole pervading decorative spirit. Enthusiasm has soared to a high pitch in the Bawdlands district where triumphal arches have been erected. In Parson Lane, too, is an "ancient" arch, which, doubtless, is intended to be in keeping with the neighbouring Castle Church street also boasts an elaborate arch, and Salford has shown its determination not to be outshone in this respect. A tour of the town reveals the fact that a large amount of time and money has been expended; all that is required to effectively show off Clitheroe's elaborate holiday garb is sunshine.

The Workhouse

The realities of daily life are illustrated in the *Clitheroe Advertiser* of 1911 by the report that a William Asquith was arrested for begging in back Chatburn Road. This man was a stranger to the town, and there had been many complaints about beggars in Chatburn Road where they were a great nuisance. The houses in Chatburn Road were recently built, and would be among the more prosperous and seen as a good place to pick up the odd shilling or item of clothing such as the pair of old boots Asquith reportedly acquired. The workhouse, locally known as *'Coplow'* now Clitheroe Hospital was still very much in evidence; in fact during the week of the festivities there were 101 people living there. In another issue of the paper, a husband and wife were sentenced to 14 days hard labour in prison - the husband was claiming to be too old to get work, and asked for them to be sent to the workhouse, instead of prison. As the town had to support them if they went to the workhouse, this option was only used if all else failed. The workhouse was closely monitored by the Board of Guardians, who met at fortnightly intervals to discuss the running of the Institution. In one newspaper report, fighting broke out and violence ensued from a row over clean handkerchiefs! The assailant claimed he had only had two clean ones in the last 12 months - this was denied by an assistant at the workhouse, who gave evidence that they were handed out every Saturday. Obviously not a soft option to end up at *'Coplow'* and not a temporary one either - it seems this particular inmate had been before the magistrates on nine previous occasions since 1900, six of them for misbehaviour at the workhouse. For this latest, he was sentenced to four months in jail with hard labour. This photograph shows Chatburn Road's arch in 1902; no mention is made of the institution further up the road which was probably a source of embarrassment to the residents of the new houses.

Marshalling the Floats

This was the fifth torchlight procession, and by now its popularity and excellence were well established. Its route this year started from Chatburn Road, where the Cricket

Bawdlands Arch in 1911

Field was called into service as the marshalling point for processionists on foot and any members of a band or group. Marshals were employed to organise them, and well in advance of the procession, the points at which floats had to assemble were worked out. The programme I have used for this particular year has pencilled notes throughout - for example the Borough of Wilkin comprising '*5 lurries and band*' had to assemble at '*Highbrake*' currently the Residential home for the Elderly opposite Clitheroe Royal Grammar School and the Whalley Road contingent were sent to the '*first lamp above Highbrake*'. The Borough of Primrose had the first spot at the entrance to the Cricket Field, and my note says that 350 torches were to be given out. What a shame the weather was so dreadful.

An interesting note at the end of the official programme informs us that special late stopping trains to Hellifield and Blackburn were laid on - to Blackburn at 11.10 pm and to Hellifield at 11.34 pm. This gives some idea of the numbers of spectators expected, and the wide area from which people came to see the festivities.

1923

The grim period of the First World War and its aftermath as Clitheroe struggled to regain some sort of normality was not the time for celebrations. Surviving from one day to the next was difficult enough - there was no enthusiasm for any more. However, by 1923 it was felt that people were now ready for a little light relief.

Clitheroe Castle

In November 1920, Clitheroe Corporation had decided to purchase the Castle and its grounds as a War Memorial for the town from the Clitheroe Estates Company. The price to be paid was £9,500 - a reasonable enough sum when one considers the human suffering and hardship which was the reason for its purchase. The Roll of Honour lists 257 men from Clitheroe and district who lost their lives. The money for this had to be raised somehow - and a Castle Fete was one way of accomplishing this, whilst ensuring that people had some very welcome fun. By 1923 the town's population had risen to over 12,000 - not much less than the 13,159 of the 1991 census.

The *Clitheroe Advertiser and Times* report of 31st August 1923 tells us that the dimensions of the procession exceeded all expectations. They even go so far as to suggest that if the torchlight procession was to become an annual event, it should be held in the afternoon, not the evening, and the torches should be abandoned in favour of daylight. The reasons for this is that the 500 torches handed out were woefully inadequate for the numbers of people taking part - electric street lighting had still not arrived, and the gas lamps were few and far between so the streets would be in darkness for the better part of the procession, which began to move off around 9 pm. The reporter points out that due to the size of the procession, the participants had to huddle together and their lavish outfits could not be seen to their best advantage. Luckily, this niggardly attitude was not shared by the townsfolk, and the tradition of the evening torchlight survives.

By now the motor lorry had made its appearance in Clitheroe, and improved the tableaux by providing a bigger space which wasn't required to be propelled by unpredictable horses, or even worse, unpredictable men! Such were the numbers in the streets, that the mounted police were necessary to clear the way - this sort of scene is difficult to imagine today - will 1999 be as well supported?

The Ku Klux Klan are represented, and maintain that they are allowed to enjoy themselves as they had travelled so far to get here! They claim to have been sent from America to maintain order during the '*Klarnival*' and are '*klamping*' on Henthorn Park, '*Klitheroe*'. The Ku Klux Klan, formed in 1866 after the American Civil War as a secret society, and wearing hoods to disguise their identity, used to ride out at night horse whipping Negroes, burning their property and murdering them if necessary. The American Congress put a stop to this, and by 1900 the movement had died down. However, after the 1914-18 war, it revived as an anti-Jewish, anti-Catholic and anti-Negros society, so the appearance of a Ku Klux Klan contingent in our torchlight Procession would have caused much consternation - we are told their raids on the crowd were '*diverting*'!

It is such a shame that not more photographs are in existence of some of the characters described in the programmes - what would the Mascotaurus look like - reputed to be a 3000 year old prehistoric animal disturbed from its beauty sleep during excavations for restorations at the Castle, or the Coplowdactyl bird? We can only speculate, I'm afraid. Although not many private individuals would have cameras in those days, there must have been some official photographers out there somewhere! However, the weight and size of the equipment would be considerable and night-time photography presumably would not be a rapid affair - it seems unlikely that the procession could stop for a photographer to ply his trade.

Reading the programme gives an idea of the size of the procession - there are over 120 separate tableaux listed, with entries still coming in. Each of these was made up of groups of several people, meaning that there must have been several hundred participants in addition to the large crowds of spectators.

The finale to this years efforts was the Firework Display from the Castle Keep. The *Clitheroe Advertiser and*

Times reports dazzling effects - including a fountain of fire, rockets emitting various coloured balls, zig-zagging rockets and a large Catherine Wheel. We can only hope that the spectators were standing well away! This year the last train, going as far as Gisburn was 11.48 pm, and for Blackburn - 11.55 pm. The reported size of the crowds means that these would be the last in a series of full trains to leave Clitheroe Station - it seems difficult to imagine now.

1924

The success of the 1923 Procession, and the continuing need to raise money for the War Memorial, prompted a repeat of the same in 1924. However lessons having been learned from the previous year when the large numbers of entrants and lack of light meant that costumes and other effects couldn't be seen, this year someone suggested holding a Fancy Dress Parade on the Castle Estate prior to the torchlight procession. Consequently the processionists were

asked to assemble on the Castle grounds at 6.30 pm, still daylight of course as it was in August. This proved a great success - both from the monetary point of view, as people were charged 6d at the entrance to the Castle field for the privilege of seeing the costumes at close quarters and from the entrants point of view as their efforts could be appreciated. There had been a Fancy Dress Ball the preceding evening, and many of these people turned out in their costumes for the competition, as well as the processionists.

Cutey Dolls and Scarecrows!

Prizes were awarded to vehicles and to people. First prize for vehicles went to a representation of a stage-coach by Mr. John Todd. The coach belonged to the late Mr. C. B. Wright, of Bolton by Bowland, and was turned into a stage coach which recalled the time when Clitheroe was a centre for stage coaches, and the Swan and Royal was a coaching house, complete with stables for the horses. There must have been a tremendous amount of work put into these

exhibits. First prize for the foot processionists went to a group of '*Cutey Dolls*'. These apparently were well known by people who had visited Blackpool, and were made from Plaster of Paris, having a baby face, round tummy, wrinkled legs, feathery sash and a big coiffure! The mind boggles - especially as the purpose of these dolls is not made clear - were they children's toys or ornaments? Well, someone from Commercial Mill had the bright idea of making human Cutey dolls, and won first prize for their efforts. The first prize for an individual entry went to a remarkable scarecrow, in the person of Mr. B. Simpson.

A photograph from the *Clitheroe Advertiser* showing the First Prize winner of the Torchlight Procession Float in 1924.

The Fancy Dress Parade set the scene for another good-humoured procession which left the Castle Field at 8.30 pm following an altered route, but still covering most of the area around the town - going as far afield as Primrose, Shawbridge and Parson Lane. The programme contains many of last years entrants, including the Mascotaurus, who was only persuaded to enter by the promise of three boy scouts and a policeman for supper! We are not told how they decided who should be the lucky foursome.

The Royal Borough of Cheshire was still very much in evidence, having acquired a banner this year, presented by Hentry VIII (!) when he opened the Brewery and gave a dissertation on '*Women I have met*' - most of them were '*cats*' he said - an appropriate connection for Cheshire. We are reminded that these mock Boroughs were originally formed as a cynical opposition to the pomposity and ceremony of the Corporations, by the following description:-

'*The Mayoral equipage will also bear the pompous and bewigged City Clerk (*a reference to the Town Clerk, William Self Weeks, often pictured wearing his lawyers wig)...*the Tacks Collector, and other officials, together with the Water Bailiff, Punch Compounder and other indispensibles on all visits to the Water Works*'

This photo shows Belle Duckworth (formerly Wrigley) as Britannia. She was part of Westhead Mill's float and chosen for her very long hair. The float was entitled '**Great Britain and her Dependancies**'. This is a particularly interesting photo as it was taken by Ralph Wrigley, Belle's brother, who became a well-known local photographer who went on to take photos for local newspapers.

- another reference to the costly and seemingly pointless Annual Waterworks Inspection.

The Royal Borough of Cheshire must have had some real wits with a way with words amongst them - their programme descriptions are always very amusing, with an almost literary turn of phrase! A later newspaper reports that the Castle Carnival made a net profit of £950, although the torchlight procession failed to cover its costs.

1935

A long gap followed the two memorial fetes; there is a limit to the amount of fund raising a small town can support, and torchlight processions are expensive in terms of labour and materials. However in 1935 the Silver Jubilee of King George V and Queen Mary couldn't be ignored and a programme of celebrations as reproduced here covering the full week of May 6th - 12th was devised. A lot of change was sweeping through Britain at the time, the country was still re-establishing itself after the horrors of the First World War, and the world wide depression of the 1930's was being felt. The mood of the people in Clitheroe seems buoyant however, as they determined to enjoy the celebrations.

The Road Traffic Act of 1934 saw the introduction of the 30mph speed limit in built up areas, an imposition not popular with the motorists of Clitheroe:

Big boy blue come blow your horn
For the 30mph limit makes motorists mourn.

The motor car was becoming commonplace now and available to many ordinary people. Adverts were beginning to appear in the paper for used cars, and the availability of reliable transport meant people were beginning to travel further afield.

Tucker's Pleasure Grounds

One of the rhymes in the programme mentions '*Tuckers Pier*', which is shown on the 1912 Ordnance Survey map as a boat house, pleasure grounds and landing stage and will be remembered by many of the older residents of Clitheroe and district. Mr. Eli Tucker set up '*Tuckers Pleasure Grounds*' providing several boats for people to sail on up and down the Ribble. Such was the popularity of this venture that at one stage he had about thirty boats in use. My own grandmother could remember walking from Accrington on Good Friday to '*Tuckers*', and told me of the huge crowds gathered there, from all over East Lancashire. There were refreshments provided by the tearooms, and swing boats for more reluctant sailors. This enterprise continued from 1876 to about 1930. Walking down by Brungerley today it seems difficult to believe, but the photograph is evidence of its popularity.

The back page of the programme gives the usual train times, but this year also gives a list of bus times to all sorts of places; the local bus service began in 1926, and was well established by 1935. The last bus to Bolton by Bowland was midnight, and Pendleton and Chaigley were 11.45pm. Those were the days!

1937

The Coronation of King George VI and Queen Elizabeth (who at 99 this year is better known as the Queen Mother) took place in 1937, after the historic abdication of Edward VII who wanted to marry Wallis Simpson, an American

A photo showing some of the boats provided by Mr. Tucker at Brungerley Bridge.

divorcee but was prevented by the Constitution. Although only two years had elapsed since the previous one, another torchlight procession had to be staged for a major event such as a Coronation.

There are several entries in this years procession from the surrounding villages - Newton and Slaidburn being just two. Their entries are amusing - they call themselves 'light and shade' referring to the fact that in 1936 Newton received electricity, but Slaidburn did not, which caused a great deal of trouble locally. It probably would have caused even more had the villagers of

Slaidburn known it was to be 1942 before they received their own supply!

This procession was the longest ever known by all accounts, and was finished off by a grand fireworks display from the Castle - this must have been quite a sight as no less than 28 types of firework are listed by name at the back of the programme.

1948

The period from 1937 to the next procession in 1948 included the Second World War. The end of the war in 1945

This float was made in 1948 by the residents of Garnett Road - the base is just an ordinary flat-backed lorry, and its theme was advertising. A tremendous amount of work must have gone into the construction of this float.

Rolls Royce's jet-propelled witches in 1948.

saw many Clitheroe families bereaved; the newspapers for the period make very sober reading- every week deaths and woundings are reported as the dreaded telegrams are delivered to the families of the servicemen. Whilst V.E. Day in 1945 heralded the end of the war, many of the local men were still on active service or imprisoned. Rejoicing on a grand scale was inappropriate at this time, although smaller events such as street parties were being held.

It wasn't until 1948 that the next torchlight procession was held to commemorate the 800th anniversary of the Charter granted by Henry de Lacy to Clitheroe. The original Charter is missing and its contents unknown, but it is referred to in a later (1283) Charter confirming 'all the liberties and customs…of the gift and grant of Henry de Lascy our ancestor'. Prior to this the whole town, buildings, land and animals would be seen as belonging to the Lord of the Manor, in this case Henry de Lacy. The Charter gave the townspeople the freedom to administer their own affairs, and for some people the right to own some of their own land. The procession celebrating this took place on August 7th 1948, and the first interesting item in the newspaper report is that there were three cinemas in the town - it is reported that the two nearest the centre of the town could only manage one customer between them and cancelled their shows, but that the other one continued with its performance, though to a much depleted audience. Once again the streets were packed with people from all over keen to join in the fun. We can see many elements of the programme which are a consequence of the Second World War, the first page is a list of 'regulations' now given a lengthy serial number as if it was a War Office publication. The first regulation is that spectators will not be more than three deep and not less than twelve inches apart and may stand easy. Secondly an application has been made to the Minister of Health for permission for spectators to breathe. Most of the other eleven regulations are along similar lines - this procession must have been a very welcome opportunity for people to let their hair down.

Rationing

In 1948 food was still being rationed and several references to this are made in the programme. Mr. Strachey who was Minister for Food in the post-war Labour government and who was responsible for prolonging rationing is referred to in less than flattering terms throughout. This poem is typical:

MR. STRACHEY'S WIZARDS

A merry medley of magicians who, with a wave of the wand can double the rations! See the bacon ration through the giant microscope!…

Mr. Strachey's Wizards
Couldn't do better
Making rice puddings
From nice soyetta;
Painting stripes on whalemeat
Imitating gammon
Colour washing snoek
To look like salmon.

The lengths people were willing to go to, to satisfy their tastebuds! This was ersatz taken to the limit. At least the Low Moor pig escaped being eaten - he has managed to reach achieve the ripe old age of $2,108\frac{1}{2}$ years - the monkey gland treatment has obviously been unavailable throughout the war.

Rolls Royce's presence in Clitheroe was represented by the Lancashire Witches seen in the photograph overleaf. Apparently in 1148 witches were broom propelled, whilst in 1948 they had graduated to

FOOD FACTS
Meet the
DUMPLING
family

MEET THE DUMPLING FAMILY with all its sweet and savoury members. They will help you with the meat ration and make your share of potatoes go round. Now that we have an extra 1 oz. margarine, we may be able to spare a little fat for our dumplings, and make them more tasty than ever.

BASIC RECIPE (for 4)

Ingredients: 8 oz. plain flour and 4 level teaspoons baking powder or 8 oz. self-raising flour, ½-1 level teaspoon salt, 1½-2 oz. cooking fat, about 6 tablespoons milk and water, or water to mix.

Method: Mix the flour, baking powder if used, and salt together. Rub in the fat and mix to a soft dough with the liquid. Shape into small balls, drop into boiling liquid and boil for 15-20 minutes, with a lid on the pan. N.B.—*For economical dumplings, omit the fat.*

VARIATIONS

SAVOURY Add ¼ level teaspoon pepper and 1-2 level teaspoons mixed dried herbs to the dry ingredients. Cook in soup or stew.

CHEESE Add 2 oz. grated cheese, ¼ level teaspoon pepper and a pinch of mustard to the dry ingredients. Cook in vegetable soup.

CURRY Add 1½-2 level teaspoons curry powder to the dry ingredients. Add to stews or soups, or cook in boiling water and serve with meat or fish.

SWEET Add 1 level tablespoon sugar to the dry ingredients and ½-1 level teaspoon mixed spice, cinnamon or nutmeg, if desired. Cook in boiling water, drain and serve with syrup sauce; or cook in boiling sweetened fruit juice, stewed fruit or diluted fruit squash and serve in the liquid in which they were cooked.

BAKED Use the recipe for sweet dumplings and roll out the 'dough to an oblong. Spread with 1 level tablespoon syrup, roll up like a Swiss roll and place in a greased pie-dish. Pour over ½ pint sweetened fruit juice (or 4 tablespoons orange squash and 2 level tablespoons syrup made up to ½ pint with water) and bake in a hot oven for 25-30 minutes. Serve hot with the syrup.

This advertisement from the *Clitheroe Advertiser and Times* shows how the local newspapers were used to promote the frugal use of the rations available - the '*economical*' version sounds particularly unappetising!

being jet propelled! This is of course a reference to the fact that there were test beds for Rolls Royce engines at Waterloo Mill, a fact rather unpopular with the surrounding residents for obvious reasons!

Several references are made to *'pre-fabs'* - the temporary houses erected on several sites in Clitheroe after the war to replace sub-standard housing and to catch up with the lack of house building throughout the long period of the war. Some of these *'temporary'* houses were not replaced or re-modelled until the 1990's! This verse sums up their structure and their popularity:

> PREFABRICATION
> *...Little dabs of mortar*
> *Elongated bricks*
> *Piled on one another*
> *Oh, what tricks.*
> *Little bits of paper,*
> *Little bits of string*
> *Stick them all together,*
> *Wedding ring!*

After the war there was a rush of sevicemen wanting to marry the fiancees they had left behind, but a shortage of housing for them to live in.

Another development in 1948 was the setting up of the National Health Service and this didn't escape the wit of the programme makers as we can see:

> NATIONAL HEALTH SERVICE
> *Now if you're sick*
> *You had best be quick*
> *And fill in the symptoms clear,*
> *On the proper form*
> *NumberX Sub/Norm*
> *With the day and the month and the year.*
> *You may learn when due*
> *That the thing for you*
> *(If you're docketed 'still alive')*
> *Is the treatment 2*
> *From the bottle blue*
> *And the pill that is number 5.*

All this was finished off by a fireworks display from the Castle Keep. An amusing story about this display is recounted by one of the four local people drafted to man the display from within the walls of the keep. At the appointed hour of 10.30 pm the first fireworks were detonated, only to scare two of the volunteers so badly that they ran off, leaving the two remaining volunteers to run the show! Luckily one of these had been in the Royal Artillery and was used to reports from ammunition and was able to continue the display, but it does make one wonder what memories were awoken in the other two, coming so soon after the ending of the Second World War.

1951

1951 was the year of the Festival of Britain and the whole country was involved in celebrations of some sort to finally lay to rest any lingering ghosts from the Second World War and to embark on a period of re-awakening for a country subdued by the events of 1939 - 1945. The announcement overleaf from the *Clitheroe Advertiser and Times* gives the details of the forthcoming procession.

The first page of the programme gives us a potted history of the torchlight processions - and the following dates should be remembered:

> *1066 - Julius Caesar landed at Brungerley.*
> *1101 - The towns bow and arrow paid for.*
> *1606 - The council resolve to make a hole in the*
> *   Castle Keep in order to attract visitors.*

So that's where it came from!

Something about to be rationed it appears is air as the poem shows:

> CLITHEROE AIR SUPPLY CO. (VERY LIMITED)
> The air bottlers.
>
> *...The air we breathe is one of the things*
> *Which hasn't been messed about.*
> *But who can doubt that a scheme so lax*
> *Is just about due for a thumping tax?*
> *So let us get busy and bottle away*
> *A bottle of air may be scarce one day.*

The announcement of the Torchlight Procession for the Festival of Britain Celebrations from the *Clitheroe Advertiser and Times*.

Investors are invited to apply for shares in a new venture to exploit the health giving properties of Clitheroe air. A modern factory has been established at Pimlico to gather, distil, bottle and market this valuable commodity...

The above verse seems to be a dig at the Labour government which had just imposed charges for dentures and spectacles, and was busy nationalising coal, gas and electricity.

Such was the scale of this year's procession that it is reported that the 300 participants took ninety minutes to pass through the streets. The leaders were the Carnival King and Queen and the Jester as usual, this year in the shape of Jimmy Fell and Sam Bridge, with Edmund Cambien as the Jester and the newspaper reports that their *'inspired humour'* got the Procession off to a good start.

1953

Tragically King George VI died in February 1952, and when the young Princess Elizabeth was crowned in June of 1953 it was felt that a torchlight procession should be held to mark the occasion. More historic events are recorded in the programme, for example in 1066 apparently *'King William I laid the foundation stone of the Castle. During the ceremony the stone fell off the rope and landed on Williams foot, at which point he exclaimed 'chacun a son gout' which is of course Lancashire for 'Right on me perishing corn!' After this he was always known as 'William the Corncurer'. This incident was also celebrated by a torchlight procession'.*

Apparently this procession was a more restrained affair than in the past - possibly due to only having a two year gap between this and the last. For some reason the Town Council, previously providing fodder for the programme makers must have been having a harmonious period and were not held to account. However the newspaper reports that it was the prettiest procession and singles out William Westheads Mill which depicted the story of the Willow Pattern plate in fabric. Jubilee Mill had made a model of Mount Everest as a tribute to the successful expedition by Sir Edmund Hillary and Sherpa

Sgt. Tom Wood proudly leads the 1953 Procession on his Police motor-cycle.

Tenzing to reach the summit of Everest earlier this year, particularly important to the mill as they wove the fabric for some of the equipment.

As this procession was held in June it was not really necessary to light it by the traditional torches in large quantities, also of course by now all the floats were on motorised wagons with headlights. However some traditional torches were still used. This year as usual there were two mounted policemen at the head of the procession, led as we can see from this photograph of the York Street area by police motorcyclist, Sergeant Tom Wood.

This year for reasons of economy, the Town Council decided not to hold the traditional ox roast, usually held at the Coronation celebrations. The decision was unpopular and two floats depicted other cheaper alternatives. one roasting a huge carton of meat extract, and another a string of pale flabby sausages. Luckily the Low Moor Pig having been stuffed and being over 1,000 years old was not considered suitable!

1960

The Castle Fete in 1960 was the starting point for the next procession - more torches this time as it was held in September when the evenings were beginning to 'draw in'. The celebrations were not for anything in particular, more the programme says as a result of spontaneous combustion, or the burning desire of Clitheroe's people for self expression.

Swinging Sixties

The beatniks of the 1960s were very much in evidence in this year's programme; England was heading for the Swinging Sixties and Clitheroe wasn't going to be left out. Grindleton Youth Group presented a float of beatniks, while Low Moor couldn't really decide what the difference was between a beatnik and a sputnik! The Catholic Youth Group organised a beatnik competition on their float, perhaps hoping to help the Low Moor contingent discover their identity.

The big news of this procession was that the Town was finally to get its Public Baths over 60 years since they were first suggested. However as yet they don't have any water in them. Still on an excavating theme, digging holes was becoming a local passion - there was an entry from the Clitheroe Corporation Highways Department entitled '*The hole in the road*'. Not much has changed! By 1960 many householders owned a car and the roads were obviously feeling the strain as were some of the older inhabitants; this heartfelt rhyme was submitted by '*two barmy old men*' (no names mentioned).

THE HORSE THAT ESCAPED FROM A ROUNDABOUT

I used to gallop round and round
But found that it made me dizzy;
Now trotting through the town is grand
Except that I can't understand
The many signs and one way streets
And why it is so busy!

The fireworks display this year was the finale for the whole of the Castle Fete celebrations, and one of the highlights was the Niagara Falls in fireworks cascading from the keep. Unfortunately there was a badly timed heavy shower of rain right at the beginning but it did little to dampen the spirits of the crowd or spoil the display of fireworks which continued for over half an hour. What a wonderful natural asset the Castle is - it could have been purpose built for firework displays!

1965

The 1965 procession is billed as a '*Quinquennial*' event - one which is held every five years. The success of previous events coupled with a period of relative economic stability meant that the time was ripe for celebrations. The programme written for the procession bears witness to some of the big changes going on locally and events which to some extent are still being felt today.

The ownership of televisions had been on the increase, and by 1965 a large percentage of households had '*the box*'. This is evident throughout the programme - in addition to '*Dr. Who*', we had '*The Black and White Minstrel Show*' from William Westhead & Sons Mill. Robinson and Spensley (egg packers) offered the theme of their float as '*Go to work on an egg*' from a TV advertisement of the time. Clitheroe Young Farmers did a '*This is Your Life*' featuring '*Bandy Shaw and the Singing Muckspreaders*'. '*Gilligans Isle*' is another familiar name paraded by Low Moor, who also performed a '*Top of the Pops*' - TV had obviously made a big impact on the inhabitants of Low Moor.

Low Moor had other events this year which were to make an even bigger impact on the inhabitants - the demolition of a lot of property in the village. At the end of 1964, the *Clitheroe Advertiser and Times* reported '*The end of a way of life*' in Low Moor. Some of the property had outlived the purpose for which it was built, that of providing housing for the hundreds of workers needed by Low Moor Mill. The mill was long since gone, and much of the housing became sub-standard. The village was far enough away from Clitheroe for it to have two chapels, a church, its own Post Office and a few shops. However, improvements enjoyed by many houses in Clitheroe were not shared by Low Moor - many still had outdoor privies, leaking roofs were common, and the spectre of a redundant mill loomed over the community. Back to back houses still existed, washing was still strung out over the street giving the area a run down appearance. The Council proposed that 60 houses should be demolished, along with the old school, an air raid shelter and various other buildings. A time of great upheaval to many followed, but the result is that Low Moor is still a

This is one of the 'Musical' floats! Notice the torches held aloft.

community, as the steward of Low Moor Club was telling me. He, with the committee of the Club, is involved in holding all kinds of events for the families who live there, and the remaining old housing is now desirable property, still affordable for young families. The new housing built on the site of the old mill is blending in with its surroundings and its residents becoming part of the community. The Club's entry in the programme:

"When you've knocked down all the houses
and the dust has cleared away.

Just think of the bright future
And get Youngers every day."

Along with the advert on the front cover for '*Low Moor Unbuilding Society - Demolish your own house!... Let our Medical Officer inspect and condemn your houses*' it gives some idea of the uncertainty of their fate felt by many.

Industry in the town seemed to be dominated by two factories which today are still some of our biggest employers - Ribble Cement as it was known then, employing nearly 500 men, and I.C.I. This cartoon overleaf is a wry reflection on the hole left by the quarrying for raw materials for cement production. This extract from the end of the verse by Clitheroe Round Table:

Blast and dig, then blast again, sincerely we intend
That when we've finished Worsaw off - God help Kemple End!
And Bleasdale Fells and Whalley Nab and Castle Keep and all,
'Til we have changed fair Ribblesdale to one big
RIBBLESHOLE!

...and the one entitled *'Lang may your lum reek'* show that even 35 years ago the company was causing controversy by its application to build a second chimney:

A lone white sentinel guards our town
Spreading white steam all o'er it;
And soon we'll hear the gladsome news
They've built a pal to join it....

" BUT THEY DID HOLD A PUBLIC INQUIRY, YOU KNOW "

A cartoon from the 1965 programme showing most of Clitheroe quarried away!

An item missing from the programme is a timetable of trains; Beeching's axe fell in 1962 and trains were absent from Clitheroe until the hard working members of Ribble Valley Rail were successful in persuading the powers that be to reinstate a regular rail service once more in 1994. This advert on the back page is amusing:

FOR SALE: 49 fancy brick Archways. Suitable for decorative garden features. Will sell singly or in lots. Buyer collects. Apply to Station Master, Whalley.

This of course refers to the Whalley Viaduct or *'arches'* as they are often referred to locally, a well known landmark and of course part of the railway line. What a good job they didn't manage to sell them!

Only the fireworks remained - these lit up the sky and silhouetted the castle against the blackness for over half an hour - a fitting end to another triumphant portrayal of life in a small market town.

1970

1970 saw the last quinquennial torchlight procession. Successive processions were held as a result of national events, as they were prior to 1960. Carnival King was again Mr. Jimmy Fell, although he intends to abdicate after this event. His Queen this year is Mr. Colin Turner - who is advised to be very careful as he is the fifth consort and the king is an admirer of King Henry VIII! Jester this year was Roger Hargreaves of joiners and French Connection fame.

This year's programme includes photographs for the first time. One of the first photographs in the programme shows a multi chimneyed factory, complete with smoke plumes, with the caption *'Doggo Food Factory'*. This was a thinly veiled reference to Dugdales, the animal food merchants who wanted to build a new factory on land very close to Ribblesdale Avenue. Clitheroe didn't have an industrial estate in 1970 - Upbrooks was built in 1979 and it wasn't until 1980 that Dugdales finally acquired their new premises on land at Salthill. Demands for increased production coupled with lack of suitable industrial land must have been a problem for several local firms at this time.

The swimming baths are almost finished this year - as the cover opposite shows - Low Moor Dairies are delivering Asses Milk and Cleopatra is said to be *'within'*. A noticeable

The lavish cover of the 1970 programme. Clitheroe eagerly awaits the opening of the Swimming Baths.

feature of this year's programme is the number of industries represented - Lucas's, Ribble Cement, Neotechnic, Lancaster Hosiery, Bowker Bros., I.C.I. William Westhead, James Thornber, Trutex, Flexible Reinforcements, Castle Castings and TGB. The fireworks display took place against a perfect night sky, providing a fitting finale to the celebrations.

1973

April 1974 is a date of great significance to any Local Government employee. It was the first day of Local Government reorganisation - when a lot of small boroughs were swallowed up by the larger County Councils. Clitheroe was no exception - Lancashire County Council devoured the old Borough of Clitheroe and took on responsibility for all its services. Added to this indignity, was the inclusion in the Ribble Valley District of Lancashire of several Yorkshire villages - the Wars of the Roses were fought all over again. Waddington, West Bradford, Grindleton and Slaidburn, along with several others, were transferred from the West Riding of Yorkshire to Lancashire. The River Ribble, formerly the County boundary was no longer a barrier between the two counties. Some 19th century maps of Lancashire show just a blank space on the other side of the river - even the Ordnance Survey acknowledged the hostility between the two counties! Feelings ran very high and there was a considerable amount of resistance and resentment. It was considered so important that a torchlight procession was held in 1973 to mark the demise of the old Borough.

I.C.I.'s entry for the 1973 procession.

Waddington Youth Club, dressed as Hillbillies, caused chaos when, on their way into Lancashire from Yorkshire, they discovered that their float would not fit under Waddington Road Bridge. They detoured via Edisford in order to reach the assembly point on time. Another Yorkshire entry was 'Sawley Races', assembled by Sawley W.I. Their steeds had four legs and rockers, and were ridden by WI members. Two opposite seasons were represented by different companies - winter by Atkinsons, who manufactured snow clearing machinery; their float took 3 weeks to make and threw out artificial snow over the crowd. I.C.I adopted a Hawaiian theme, as shown with 'Calypso Island' featuring dusky maidens wearing flowered garlands and palm trees galore.

The Low Moor Pig made his appearance with Lord and Lady Bacon, protesting at local government reorganisation; Low Moor wanted to declare their independence and form their own Parish Council. The picture opposite shows Lord and Lady Bacon with Percy, being presented with a pig's head on a platter.

The BBC filming the Low Moor Pig in 1973. Lord and Lady Bacon are respectively Mrs. Stella Wilson (formerly Cutler) and Alan Dixon. Edith Child, wife of the local butcher, is presenting the pig's head, watched by William Hargreaves and Raymond McQuarrie.

Not all was plain sailing and fun - an articulated lorry in the procession suffered brake failure, scattering the watching crowds in York Street, The fault proved temporary, and no-one was injured. Also, the firework display from the Castle Keep was marred by *'unauthorised persons'* going up to the Keep and interfering with the proceedings. However, a half hour display was still provided, with the public being largely unaware of the disruption.

So, the old Borough went out in a blaze of glory, having continued the tradition of the torchlight procession for 86 years. Would the new Borough Council be able to maintain the tradition?

1977

Queen Elizabeth II was the second monarch in 100 years to celebrate her Silver Jubilee, and 1977 was also the year that saw so little support for a pageant in Clitheroe to celebrate the Queen's Silver Jubilee that it had to be scrapped. Was this a reflection on the watering down of Clitheroe's identity and its loss of status, or just, as seems more likely a sign of the times, and the impact of the arrival of electronic entertainment?

However plans for staging another torchlight procession continued. On reading the programme and the newspaper report it is obvious that there was

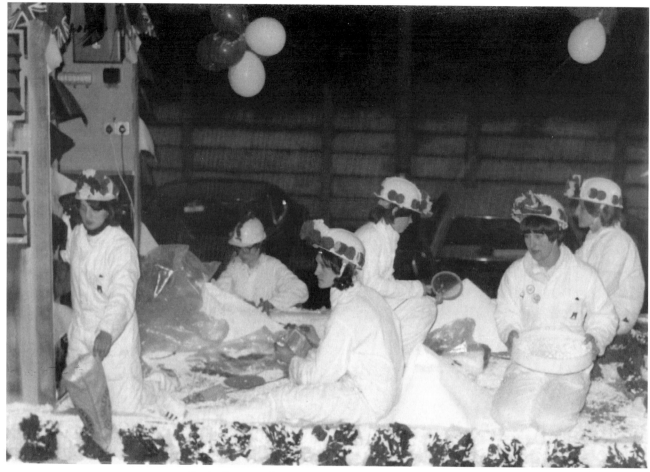

Castle Cement sifting lumps from their cement in 1977.

no watering down of enthusiasm for the tradition. This year saw record entries and a superb programme; somewhere feelings of civic pride were still running strong - even the firework display was unparalleled! Some of this of course could be attributed to feelings of patriotism for a popular Queen, but much is due to the simple fact that the strong community spirit pervading Clitheroe endures major changes. It is possibly even further strengthened, dare I say, by the acquisition of our Yorkshire neighbours, who seem to have entered into the spirit of the occasion regardless of former boundaries and hostilities. The introduction to the programme expresses worry that in 1974, having been disintegrated into Ribble Valley (and going to pieces ever since) and losing all their pet jokes, pet topics and pet councillors, no fodder would be available to base the processions programme on. However Ribble Valley Council rushed to their aid and came up with some *'cracking good ideas'*.

There were 87 floats in this year's procession - a record number, and all went very smoothly and fluently. In addition to the floats were bands, Morris dancers and pedestrian entries. The nearest estimate the newspapers could manage of the number of spectators was between 10,000 and 25,000! The route of three miles was lined up to 10 people deep at some points. That's almost as big as the gate at some Blackburn Rovers Football matches- admission is free too!

One of the RVBC's bright ideas was to pedestrianise the town centre, by means of another by-pass. The idea was short-lived, but provided fodder for *'mickey taking'*. The Chief Planning Officer is quoted as saying *'By next year they will be operating on my southern and western internal by-passes'*. *'You should feel a lot better for that, lad'* interjected Dame Myra. Another bright idea was to try to close the Auction Mart which prompted Clitheroe Lady Farmers to plead *'E don't try to close R auction'*. It took a further 10 years for this plan to reach fruition. A plaintive poem entitled *'Ribble Valley Rules O.K.'* has a double page spread lamenting the intrusion of Councillors from other areas into their affairs, including wanting to build a tripe factory at Crosshills! Actually, this was not so far fetched as it sounds - there used to be a small brick built factory at Crosshills with a large chimney, used for the preparation of tripe; located here as it was a long way from any dwellings in the 19th century. The remains of the building were visible up until the middle of this century. Castle Cement offered the motto *'Graded grains make finer cement'* - the photograph opposite shows them busily sifting!

William Westhead's Mill again submitted a lavish float, pictured here. It was modelled on the Tutenkhamun Exhibition

Westhead's workers dressed for their Tutenkhamun float.

which caused a sensation in London. The fabric for the costumes was all woven at the mill - the silver fabric which many of the costumes were made from was actually the same as that used for the silver flags which lined the Mall in London for the Queen's Silver Jubilee. The Tutenkhamun exhibition was viewed by the mill owner when he visited London on business and he provided the idea for the float

1981

The wedding of Prince Charles to Lady Diana Spencer was in July 1981 and took place amidst much pomp and ceremony in St. Paul's Cathedral. Clitheroe's celebration of the event was a much less formal affair - in fact some could call it almost disrespectful! This year's programme writers again excel themselves; there is far too much to quote here, but we must include some nuggets of wisdom.

The poem written in dialect about Charles' visit to Clitheroe is so good that it seems worth reproducing in full.

CHARLES BEWITCHERED

When Charlie were first asked to visit
He had a quick chat with 'is Dad,
His first words were *"Where the 'ell is it?"*
And 'is Dad said *"Nay lad, arta mad?"*
"It's up yon in't Ribblesdale Valley
All gulleys and channels and drains,
Thi Mother'll swear thar Dulally-
And what will ta do if it rains?"

His Mum said *"It's damper ner Bacup,*
Nowt yonder but drizzle and bogs,
Tha'd better ring Alben Snape up
And see if he'll lend tha 'is clogs;
And tha'd best put thi red flannel vest on,
To ward off thi' rheumatic pains,
Cos once tha gets far side o' Preston
I'll lay six to four as it rains!"

"When I were at Wadda" said Maggie,
"Inspecting their tent and latrine,
Mi Royal Regalia went mouldy
And all t' little Brownies turned green.
I've 'ad drier fortneets i' Venice,
It's hissed down in Spain on the Plains,
It's rusted the hooks off me bodice,
I feel fair let down when it rains!"

"I'll sail up i' Brittania an' park it."
Said Prince as he started to pack
"I've that black rubber suit frae th'Antartic
And I'll tek 'Arold Wilson's owd mac,
There's that hat wi' the corks round frae Aussie,
And that brolly o' Nev Chamberlains,
And wi' Gret Uncle David's owd cossie
I'll be ready for owt if it rains…

Prince Charles had in fact visited the area in May 1981 and went to Calderstones Hospital as part of his tour of the North West.

The Civic Hall has been in trouble again this year. The building was found to be listing at an unacceptable angle and the rear wall was shored up for some time. There is a *'spoof'* article from a *'resident'* of Pisa who is in Clitheroe on a *'paccheg'* holiday, likening the Civic Hall to his own leaning tower. Eventually £65,000 was spent on repairs to the building, leading to exactly the same discussions as are going on as I write; falling audiences and the amount of money spent on subsidising each ticket. Some things never change!

Another topic providing fodder for the programme was the building of the new Council Offices. There was a good deal of public opposition to the building at an estimated cost of £1m. They were finally built and opened in 1980. This extract from a poem in the programme seems to sum up local feeling about the design:

'They appointed a man to come up with a plan
Based on the Castle at Colditz.'

The winners of this year's prize for the best float went to the French Connection for their *'French Revolution'*. An ingenious design, it was manned by can-can girls and musketeers. The centrepiece was a working guillotine which occasionally chopped off a *'head'*, actually a bag stuffed with sawdust. One of these was chopped off at an inopportune moment and hit Mr. David Waddington, now Lord Waddington who was one of the judges! It obviously didn't affect his final decision.

The celebrations were ended by a dazzling display of fireworks from the Castle Keep at 10.30pm. The police are

The French Connection's French Revolution in 1981. Note the 'Guillotine'.

reported as saying they were delighted at the way things went and no trouble was reported. What a shame the royal marriage didn't follow such a smooth path!

1986

Clitheroe Castle has always been the focal point of the town both geographically - it lies in the centre of the town when looking at a map, and visually - its position on top of a limestone knoll means that it can be seen from all over the town. It is the town's war memorial commemorating the bravery of those who lost their lives during World War 1.

During the summer it is often the site of music festivals which provide entertainment for all. The Museum which educates both local people and visitors on the history of Clitheroe and the surrounding area is located in one of the Castle buildings, and there are football pitches, tennis courts, bowling greens and a large playground for young children, providing sporting and recreational facilities for all. Its gardens and grounds have been the haunt of courting couples for many years, and a visit to the top of the keep on a fine day provides one with breathtaking views of the surrounding area. In one way or another, for young and old, the Castle is a part of the lives of everyone who lives here. So it seems appropriate that in 1986 the 800th anniversary of the building of the Castle should be celebrated by a torchlight procession.

The front cover of the programme depicts a drawing of the Castle with the numbers '799' written in large numbers. '799'? Hold on, was this programme an advance edition? No, in fact this was a reference to the fact that some people disputed the year in which the Castle reached its anniversary, and some public discussion took place, but it was decided to continue the celebrations.

A New Library

The programme adopts its usual scurrilous style and is full of digs at local happenings. One of the biggest events in the town at the time was the sale of the old Clitheroe Town Hall, formerly the Moot Hall, where many important decisions have been taken over the years. The purchasers were Lancashire County Council who had acquired the site to extend the library premises. There had been years of debate about the best site for a new library. The old building was much too small to cater for the growing population and the demands put on it by a population eager for knowledge and entertainment. At one stage the Civic Hall building was suggested as a joint use site, resolving the problem of under use of the building, but this scheme fell by the wayside at the last minute. Finally, after many options were explored the Town Hall was purchased and the library's future was secured. As you can see from the illustrations, the alternative suggestions show that we had a lucky escape! The resulting conversion was a very difficult project for the architects, and

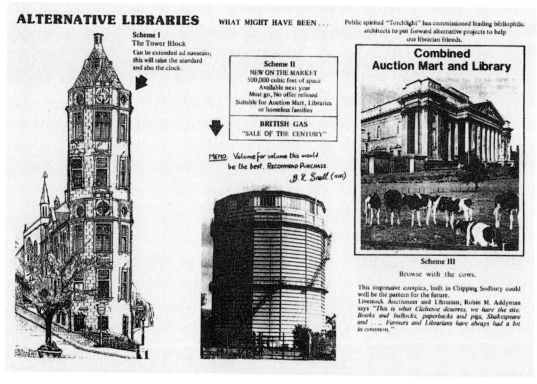

Some alternative Library schemes!

The French Connection's 'Load of Beaux!' in 1986.

the library was removed lock, stock and barrel to the United Reformed Church Hall whilst the conversion took place. The entrance to the building is down a precipitous cobbled slope, although once inside was on one level so in some ways was easier to negotiate. However issues fell and there was an added inconvenience of dreadful smells pervading the building. These were finally identified as rats decomposing under the floor, necessitating the lifting of the floor on several occasions. However the staff did sterling service in their smelly subterranean surroundings, and finally moved back into their refurbished premises in 1990. The resulting library is one of the showpieces of the County Library Service and attracts many favourable comments from visitors and locals alike.

French Connection

Clitheroe's connection with its twin town Rivesaltes has lasted well since its formation in 1978. The French Connection is the organisation which is responsible for the continuing success of the cross Channel partnership and their float was a testament to the wit, style and ingenuity of its members. It won first prize in the competition for best float, and is described in the programme as '*a load of Beaux*' It was manned by '*French*' characters such as the drunken '*Beau Jolais*' and his accountant '*Beau Nus*' who was paying too much attention to the transvestite '*Beau Derek*'. '*Beau Legs*' fell over and was refused assistance by '*Beau Nidol*'! Their float was based on the French Foreign

Legion and featured a troupe of sand and belly dancers with Roger Hargreaves popping up as Indiana Jones, complete with thunder and flashing lights. They even had an electrically operated camel whose eyes lit up and whose neck swayed in time to the music of '*Egyptian Reggae*' which was a popular tune at the time. After the procession had ended the camel was apparently left overnight in someone's garden peering over the hedge. The milkman must have had quite a shock!

Reference was made in the programme to events in the news in 1986; the introduction of the £1 coin to replace the old £1 note, the impoverished state of the N.H.S., the creation of the Sinclair C5 - whatever happened to that? Acid rain and its effects were being felt and discussed in detail nationally. Anneka Rice paid a '*surprise*' visit to the Castle by helicopter during a rehearsal for the Pageant in pursuit of a clue for the popular television programme '*Treasure Hunt*' and this event occupies two pages of the programme - it must have caused quite a stir! Arthur Scargill's name appears in one of the contributions; the miners strike had ended in 1985 after a bitter battle causing much hardship to the miners and their families. How quickly we forget events which at the time seem so important.

A total of 112 floats entered this years procession all of whom had gone to great lengths to contribute to a spectacle which wound its way round the town for about three miles and was over a mile in

VISITORS PLEASE NOTE:-

Emergency sanitary provision will be positioned this year in a newly excavated section of The Castle moats. There will also be an overflow provision elsewhere.

Moore's Terracotta army!

total length. The usual mammoth firework display from the keep of the Castle, the subject of this years procession concluded an evening of enjoyment for all.

1992

At the end of the 1986 procession Peter Moore, a member of the torchlight committee was quoted in the newspaper as saying it would be 1991 before there was another, unless there was a Royal Wedding, a Jubilee or an abdication! Well, 1991 came and went without a historic occasion to justify the work and expense of a torchlight procession. So, in desperation the 40th anniversary of Queen Elizabeth II's accession to the throne was used as the next excuse.

This 20th torchlight procession was watched by crowds estimated to be about 50,000 People from all over the North West have come to be regular watchers of these spectacular events unmatched by any other town within at least a twenty mile radius. The programme this year is sponsored for the first time by local companies advertising themselves at the foot of each page. In the past, local companies have been very generous in their support of the procession but this is the first appearance of advertising. On the page opposite is a sample of the adverts!

This year's King is Bill Taylor with John Turner playing the Queen and Edward Worswick playing the Jester as he did last time. This trio (not always the same people!) appears in each procession leading the way and zipping off into the crowd at regular intervals performing various antics and involving the spectators. It seems that the Council were less controversial at this time - the biggest 'dig' is at the decision to put a sculpture of a bull in the planned new market, on the site of the old Auction Mart, resited in 1987 to the industrial estate at Lincoln Way after being in the centre of the town for over 100 years. Many felt the design for the new market to be inappropriate for Clitheroe, and the original plans were altered fairly radically to provide the market we see today. Since its opening in May 1995 the market has been dogged by situations which have affected the traders in various ways,

not all of them within the Council's control. Bad weather during the construction and the months following the opening, particularly the summer of 1998, rows amongst some of the long standing traders and the councils attempt to introduce a third market day have all contributed to a less than harmonious market community.

The other major player in this years programme was the European Community and the introduction of the Single Market, aimed at speeding up the growth of the European economy and facilitating trading between the member states. This page from the programme shows just what fascinating jobs could be available to us once the single market has opened. I don't seem to remember any of those overleaf appearing in the *Clitheroe Advertiser and Times* though!

According to the programme the fireworks display at the end of the procession was the biggest and most expensive ever staged. The company responsible for staging it had recently won the Monaco International Fireworks display and were using several of the same type of fireworks used in their winning display. The finale was to be a set piece of the Queen, a fitting finale to a celebration of 40 years as reigning monarch.

There were reports in the national newspapers last year that the Queen had expressed a wish to retire to the Ribble Valley. I think she's heard about the way we celebrate Royal occasions and wants to be a part of the action. Who knows, the Carnival King and Queen for the torchlight procession of 2002, the Queen's Golden Jubilee could be none other than the Queen and Prince Philip! I wonder who they would choose as their Jester?

Whilst preparing this book two things became obvious; first how little written information is available on the subject; other than the official programmes and the local newspaper reports, despite appeals in the latter. Secondly, how everyone in the town who has ever witnessed a torchlight procession has their own recollections. I have attempted to use all three of these sources. However I am conscious that whilst reading this many people will have their own ideas of what should have been included.

OPPORTUNITIES IN EUROPE

A variety of interesting jobs are now open to applicants from Britain.. We invite applications for the following positions.

BOLOGNA
Spaghetti elasticity tester: must be physically strong and have own teeth. No applicants pasta sell-by date.

BRUGES
Brussel Sprout taster: needs large house and understanding family.

THE BLACK FOREST Lumberjack wanted - ideal for someone cutting down on cakes.

MILAN
Supervisor for Gorgonzola Mountain (official E.C. post). Would suit retiring personality. Although we can't have enough Jungfraus only a maggot could love this mountain! The olfactorily disadvantaged may be especially suitable. This is an equal opportunity position. *PLEASE*, somebody, take this job.

COGNAC
See photograph. Strong head and flexible backbone essential. Guaranteed a barrel of fun.

Cognac testers at the end of another hard working day.

Some of these jobs sound quite interesting!

Reading the programmes has almost been a history lesson in itself; they provide a fascinating insight into the daily life of a small rural town and the outside influences affecting it. Social history is made of events like this, unfortunately many people underestimate the value of items such as family photographs and many are destroyed. Official programmes are invaluable but were written before the event, newspaper reports appear up to a week later and awaken memories, photographs capture the mood of the moment and the spontaneity of events and should never be thrown away!